Volume X of the 20th Century Sermons Series

steps to life

BY
lynn anderson

Published By
BIBLICAL RESEARCH PRESS
774 East North 15th Street
Abilene, Texas
79601

STEPS TO LIFE
By Lynn Anderson

◇

Copyright © 1977
Biblical Research Press

◇

Library of Congress Catalog Card No. 77-20518
I. S. B. N.–0–89112–310–5

◇

Dedicated

to

two Godly parents,

one loving wife

and

four precious children

PREFACE

Aside from a Master's Thesis, this is my first attempt at a book. These sermons touch some most oft-repeated thoughts from twenty years of attempting to preach.

No art or erudition mark these messages. The pages simply state my understanding of basic concepts which are meaningful to me.

For that material which I recognize as borrowed, I have given credit. To those I plagiarized so long ago that the material seems original to me, I offer advanced apologies.

Special thanks to some precious people, Diane Church and Joyce Clemons, who have worked long and patiently typing transcriptions and manuscripts.

This material goes to print prayerfully. May anything hurtful be quickly forgotten. If anything is helpful, may it bless some life.

For Jesus,

Lynn Anderson
Abilene, Texas
December 17, 1976

CONTENTS

STEPS TO LIFE

NEWS

A WORLD WITHOUT CHRIST

This week I had a sad experience. At one sitting I read all the way through a copy of *Newsweek*. The bad news comes through clearly. Of course, there was a long story about Watergate, the personal tragedy in the lives of each of the people affected by this, the careers wrecked, the families broken. A pall of gloom has settled across the country. People have lost confidence in government. Government officials have revealed too much "humanity." Shadows lie over the president himself. Confidence of the American people is deeply shaken.

Another was a story about Israel. Twenty-five years ago a great new dream of hope began. People and money flooded there from all over the world. "A new start for God's chosen people" in their promised land.

But the years have bogged it down in economic disorder and chronic border disputes with the Arabs and Lebanese. Some who fled from Russia to Palestine are now trying to get back into Russia. So the dream is beginning to shatter!

I read the reviews of current novels. Many, without plot, are simply more sordid, miserable, wallowing in the suffering of humanity.

The "movie critique" section? The same thing. Music? Virtually the same. Nothing real was said to encourage anyone.

Stuffed in between these things were multi-colored promises of happiness if you buy the right automobile, right perfume, the right liquor, or the right soap. Or, in case that doesn't work, why, escape through television (ultra-color, even!).

I won't bore you with any more of this. It was sobering.

1

I laid the magazine aside and thought, "I wonder if we aren't beginning to find out what it's like to live in the absence of Jesus—*a world without Christ.*"

Several years ago, I said something like this to a man who replied hotly, "Well now, surely you are not going to tell me Jesus has really made any difference! He may be all right for people who need that kind of thing, but *what real difference has Jesus ever made to the world?*"

When I was a child, we often went for a drive on Sunday afternoons. The car was old. When it was hot and dusty and the road was bumpy and we kids would complain, mother would say, "All right, Dad, let's turn around and take them back home." That silenced us. Somehow even though it was hot and dusty and bumpy, we'd rather be out for a *drive* than to go back.

When someone tells me that they don't really see any contribution that Jesus had made to the world, I want to say, "Let's just turn around and look back at the world without Christ. The contrast will show us what Jesus has done."

So let's take a trip back into history to see what it was like before Jesus came. It would be naive to affirm that it was all black. I'm sure there were reasonably happy people back there. There were, of course, many worshippers of our Father, of God. But the world *was* a dark place.

PRE-CHRISTIAN WORLD

Look for awhile first at the Roman empire before Jesus came. It was, of course, co-mingled with the Greek cultural structure. For example, there was no concept of decent morality during the declining days of Greece. Then the Romans picked up and magnified the sins of the Greeks.

SEXUAL DEGENERACY

For example, the Greek Demosthenes said, "We keep

mistresses for pleasure and concubines for the day to day needs of the body, but we have wives in order to produce children legitimately."[1]

Juvenal, the Roman poet said, "Hiberina" (Hiberina was at that time the wife of the Emperor-LA) "will no more be satisfied with one man than she would be satisfied with one eye."[2]

Seneca, the Roman poet, said, "Chastity in Rome is simply proof of ugliness. Innocence is not *rare*. It's *non-existent.*"[3]

Then Juvenal again said, "The Roman woman passes the altar to modesty with a cynical smile on her face."[4]

Gibbon, in his long history of Rome, said concerning the homosexuality that had run rampant through the Empire, "Of the first fifteen Roman Emperors, Claudius was the only one whose taste in love was entirely correct."[5]

You think about that—the first fifteen Roman Emperors!

CHEAP VALUE ON LIFE

Moving next to the concept of human life: Slavery was the order of the day. Those who happened to have the upper hand, materially or politically, were masters of the others. It didn't matter that masters may be the illiterate and the crude and the slaves polished, educated and sensitive.

When the Greeks took a country, the strongest and most intelligent people of that country became their slaves. They said, "The Greeks are the only people in the world who are right to be masters." The Norsemen of the colder climates had strong bodies, but very weak minds. People south, by the equator, had strong minds, but in that climate, weak bodies. The Greeks, however, who lived in the moderate climate were the only ones who had that perfect balance of mentality and body to be the rulers of the world, as they thought.

MERCY WAS MINIMAL

In pre-Christian days the concepts of kindness and gentleness were virtually non-existent. In fact, kindness, in those days, was regarded as *weakness.* One Roman soldier wrote to his wife. He hadn't been home in awhile. His name is Hilarian and her name is Alis.

"Hilarian, to Alis:

> Greetings. Know that we are still even now in Alexandria. Do not fidget if I stay in Alexandria. I beseech you, take care of the little child, and as soon as we have our wages I will send you something. When you are delivered, if it is a male let it live, if a female cast it out. How can I forget you? So don't fidget."[6]

Sweet and gentle, isn't it!

We expect to know people we can trust, people who have sensitive love and feeling toward us, moral decency and so forth. Those of us who have grown up in a Christian climate take those things for granted. But such were extremely unusual in the days before Jesus.

THE ART OF FAITH

Look into *Europe* before Jesus came. It's difficult for us even to think about Europe without thinking about Christianity. Most of our North American Christian influences come from Europe. But, when the apostle Paul had converted many among the barbarians of the Mediterranean coast, England and Scotland and Ireland were still totally "un-Christianized." In fact, there was a common meat delicacy. It wasn't mutton, it wasn't goat, it was *shepherd's hocks.* That's right. They sometimes cooked and ate tender little shepherd boys. Occasionally, in celebrations, they drank wine from bowls made of human skulls. These were our forebears, the Anglo-Saxons, before they were touched by the influence of Jesus.

Note the changes that came to Europe. Even the skyline changed. Beautiful cathedrals (granted: it may have been misspent money) were built in an attempt to honor Jesus Christ. The art that comes from Michelangelo and Leonardo da Vinci conveys their concepts of God and of Jesus. The same is true of poetry and music.

Even the institutions for betterment of children were begun because Jesus had put his gentle hand on the child's head, giving him value.

Women are treated now, not as subordinates or sex objects, but as partners in life in European society. The profession of nursing came through a *wonderful lady;* Florence Nightingale. All this is through the influence of Jesus direct and indirect, but touching the lives of people.

Some years ago Henry Wallace wrote a play entitled, "The Eclipse of Faith." In this play, all traces of Jesus have suddenly vanished from history. In a closing scene, the principal character, a lawyer, opens a bookcase, and notices that most of the books have just a few lines scattered on the pages. The influence of Jesus had just vanished from the books. He places a record on his old victrola. Silence! Much of the music is gone because the concepts that came through the influence of Jesus have vanished. He opens his law books, then begins to tear them from the shelves, finding page after page blank. He reaches frantically for a book of poetry. There is nothing in it! He looks to the walls where his paintings have been and many of them are gone. Finally he sinks to a chair and sobs. When he catches his breath, he says, "I would not want to live in a world where there was no Christ." And then, fortunately, he awakes to find that it's just a dream.

Are *we* living in a world without Christ?

AMERICA WITHOUT JESUS

Contemplate America before the influence of Jesus came. Have you ever thought of what it would be like if you could turn back the calendar to the primeval state of this continent, totally change the characters, then update things again. What if it were a continent peopled, not by believers, but someone from Mars or someone from the Orient? Even the names of many of our cities would be different. St. Joseph, St. Louis, Los Angeles, St. Petersburg?

Or the names of the people! Where did these names come from—Matthew, Mark, Luke, John, Peter, Andrew, James, Philip, Bartholomew—common names that we give our children. (Did you know that in this country there are supposed to be 6 million women who answer to the name of Mary? And one out of every twelve males answer to the name of John.) What would our names be if Jesus had not touched American history?

Think of the educational systems of this country. The idea of public education itself came through the Christian value of every individual. Out of some 2,000 institutions of higher education, more than 800 of them began directly as institutions for Christian education. (Of course, we use "Christian" in the broad sense of the word.) Names? Harvard, Yale, University of Chicago. These all began as religious institutions under the influence, however indirectly, of Jesus Christ.

If you really want to get a feeling of what this continent might be without these influences, sometime find the darkest room you know of in an old basement. Take with you one match and one candle. Go into that dark room, shut all of the doors and the windows, wait until midnight and sit for an hour or two letting the darkness soak into your psyche. When you have had about all you can stand, strike the match and light the candle! Then you begin to appreciate the kind of contrast that's come into the world by the influence of Jesus.

WHERE JESUS HAS NEVER GONE

Now let's take a trip, not back into time, but abroad to the areas of the world where the influence of Jesus has never been very strongly felt. An old Quaker once said, "If thee would study comparative religions, do not buy thee a book, buy thee a ticket."

So "buy thee a ticket" and go, for example, to China, one of the oldest continuing civilizations in the world of which we know. What has been there for centuries? In many ways a very high order of civilization. But on the other hand, there is overpopulation; there are high disease rates. Even with the economic progress, China lags far behind many of the countries of the world where men have had the initiative and the inter-mutual concern that comes through knowing Jesus Christ.

One of the first missionaries from our fellowship to China tells this story. One day he and his wife were taking the garbage to the dump. They stumbled over a sack and the sack started to cry. When they shook out it's contents they found a baby girl that someone had left at the garbage dump to die. This is in the lifetime of our contemporaries!

Buy another ticket to India, another of the most ancient continuing civilizations in the world. Again a rich heritage. In fact, the Indians are quick to remind the West that while we were still barbarians, they had a high and sophisticated civilization. This is true. But today in India you can walk down the streets of Calcutta and you will see children and aged people lying outdoors to die. They beg for food, and people simply step over their bodies to move on. There are no institutions, government sponsored or church sponsored (at all comparable with Christian nations) to care for the lepers, the starving, the suffering. These are simply accepted as "fate." Because of the religious concepts prevalent there for centuries, folks simply don't believe in interfering in another's suffering.

A good deal of India's starvation doesn't really need to be if the arable land were cultivated. If the religious values were different, probably the sacred cows wouldn't eat the cabbage, and the people could have beef and cabbage every day! Yet, people are starving to death.

It is the cultural overlag, born of a Christless religion, which impairs India's care for those who suffer.

We could go on, picturing countries where the influence of Jesus has not really had a very broad impact. But now let's take one more glimpse at another kind of picture—our present-day world, a world where the influence of Jesus once had a heyday, but is now beginning to fade.

A WORLD WHERE JESUS IS FORGOTTEN

Probably a good place to begin would be Eastern Europe. There was a time when religion was strong in Russia and the people knew Jesus Christ. Later all they knew was the wicked priest! The church became corrupt and abused the people badly. The power structures of church and state became closely aligned. The country was ripe for the rebellion that became Communist Russia, the Soviet Republic. Jesus had left. Yes, there were churches there and there were priests, but Jesus was gone from them. Compassion was gone. Concern was gone. Gentleness was gone. Love was gone. All of the beautiful things that Jesus puts in life flickered low.

Things have changed, not all for the good. That big wall (with the machine gun nests on top) through the middle of Berlin isn't for nothing! If life is utopia behind the iron curtain, why do people frequently risk running past machine guns to get to something better. It is a world where Jesus is banished!

AMERICA

But stop and look at America! Could it be that we here in America, (back to *Newsweek* magazine), are living in a country where the influence of Jesus is rapidly vanishing? We say the name, we have the shell, and even high leaders in government pray and evoke the name of God. But the dominant value systems of America are anything but Christian. Could it be that our worship of Erotica, the goddess of sex, in this country is because somehow institutions that are supposed to be Christian have lost their impact? Could it be that we have come to mistrust most men in positions of authority, because Jesus is leaving the country? In our large cities, people don't dare go on the streets at night. They have bar locks on their doors. They can't get enough policemen to control the hostility and the tension between people. Could this be the loss of the influence of Jesus?

There was a time in America when you knew your neighbor and you could trust him. Your neighbor would care for you if you were sick, and you could care for him. There was a time when a leader in government was someone to be respected, not just envied, suspected and pampered because of his power. But that time is nearly gone!

A MAN WITHOUT JESUS

After we have done our moaning about these vast masses of the population, we'd better be realistic. What's going on in China, Russia, India or back in the Roman empire or in *Newsweek* magazine is not the issue. It's you and me as individuals.

Some years ago a little boy slipped up beside his father as he was reading the daily paper. The little boy had something he wanted to talk about. His daddy wanted to be rid of him, so he dug up an old map of the world, cut it up in little pieces like a puzzle and said, "Here son, put this map together and then come back and talk to me." He thought he'd have the paper done by then. But in a few minutes the little boy came back. He had the map all together perfectly. The father said, "Son, how did a little fellow like you know how to put the world together like that?" The reply? "Well, Daddy, there was a picture of a man on the back, and when I put the *man* together properly I found the *whole world* came out right."

The real issue is not what's going on in the *world* but what's going on in *me*. What is the picture of man without Christ?

In the *first place,* he is a man whose *struggles are futility!* Every attempt that he makes to lift himself somewhere is futile . . . even if he gets there. If he gets the million dollars that he's after, what happiness can it buy him? What peace does it give him? He's only hungering for more, or afraid he'll lose what he has. What good is it to become the most famous person in the world if one can contribute nothing to himself or to those around him? If he never discovers how to die, what has life given him?

A man in California last year who had everything, materially, came home from the office to discover that some rowdies were driving down the street and felt like shooting somebody. So they shot his three-year-old girl with a double-barreled shotgun as she sat in the front yard. He arrived just in time to pick her up as she was whimpering and dying. What did he have with which to handle that kind of a situation? His struggle is futility.

Remember graduating from high school? I was terrified at graduation. I hated school with a purple passion. But I was scared to death that I'd get stuck in some routine job that I would hate, yet would have to keep to stay alive until old age brought me to a grave. I couldn't bear that!

Every attempt is futile. Pure nothing. When you reach your goal, it's nothing. One can stand tomorrow with a brand new college diploma in his hand and say, "I worked my heart out for this. It was my 'key to life.' And now I feel just as empty and dead as I did yesterday."

MISERY

Also, after awhile, *his existence becomes misery.*

We have a way of ruining and breaking ourselves by trying to find that little glint of happiness somewhere. What we think is enjoyment and amusement, after awhile becomes sorrow and abusement. We destroy what little chance we have of putting the pieces together. When we are seized by the North American compulsion to be "happy." That's not

how we get happy. In fact, it is the road to wretchedness.

I have a little poem that I want to read, written by a man named Kagawa. He learned about Jesus when he was going to a religious university in Japan. Kagawa was serious about his faith. He began sharing with people. He was bringing beggars off the street; criminals, prostitutes, . . . into his room at the Christian university. They ejected him from the school saying, "You can't practice that kind of religion around here."

He went down to the slums of Tokyo and built a little shack out of cardboard and carpet. He would sleep there, but all day long he would look for people to whom he could minister and share good news.

One night he cared for a man in his shack who had been stabbed several times. Another night he cared for a woman and her daughter, both of them prostitutes, who had been beaten half to death by some of their customers. They died before morning.

He sat there wondering! "Where are all of these good people up on the hill?" "When are they going to help?" And then he wrote this poem.

> "I came to bring
> God to the slum;
> But I am dumb,
> > Dismayed;
> > Betrayed
> > By those
> Whom I would aid;
> > Pressed down,
> > So sad
> > I fear
> > That I am mad.
> > Pictures
> Race through my brain
> > and lie
> > Upon my heart.
> Pictures like this:
> > A man's
> legs rotted off

With syphilis;
And yet,
He need not fret
That money
Does not come
Because his wife
Is rented out
And brings
Sufficient sum.
One month in the slums,
And I am sad,
So sad
I seem devil-possessed,
or mad.
. . . here are the slippery streets, which are never dry;
They are lined with open sewers, where rats come out to
die;
Tattered paper doors stand wide to winds that beat;
The houses are all of a reddish black, like the hue of stale
whale meat;
Filth on the flimsy ceilings, dirt in the musty air;
Elbowed out of their crowded rooms, people are every-
where;
All night long they crouch in the cold, huddled on broken
benches,
Where there's never a moment's lifting of the heavy awful
stenches.
The painted idiot-girl,
upon whose back
Vile pictures
Were tattooed
In red,
Will never lure men to her den again;
She is dead . . .
You ordinary folk
Upon the hill,
To whom
The slums are vague,
Listen and tremble
As I scream to you,
'She DIED OF PLAGUE!!!'
I hear a harsh voice
Cry out,
'Here you! Dance!!'

I see a thin child dodge
And I know
It is the boy
Whose father kicks him.
Twelve years old,
Driven from bed
Into the streets,
Naked and cold . . .
I must be done with thoughts like these!
The raindrops patter from the eaves;
The fire beneath my half-boiled rice is out!
I hear the rising roar of ribald shout
That brings the evening to Shinkawa Slum.

IS THERE NO WAY
THAT HELP CAN COME?![7]

You see, this was written out of a man's experience when he touched man without Christ!

LOST

Not only is his existence misery and his struggle futility, but his *condition is lost*.

Jesus said, "I told you that you would die in your sins, for you will die in your sins unless you believe that I am he." *(John 8:24)*. *Acts 4:12* says, "And there is salvation in no one else, for there is no other name under heaven given among men by which we must be saved."

Jesus comes into the picture and things are different. My life is not like that, but I know people who grew up in parallel circumstances to me whose lives are like that. The only difference is that somehow through the grace of God, I've come to know Jesus Christ as the Lord of my life. I am able to believe in people, and believe in God, and accept and give love, and to know the meaning of sensitiveness and kindness and joy and peace. Unless I am self-deluded, I am ready any day to meet death, looking it squarely in the eye. I praise God for that.

Some years ago in Chicago a Christian family had a daughter. They were a very wealthy family. They sent their daughter away to finishing school. She was *finished,* all right. She learned how to dress properly and how to speak properly. She also learned how to hold a wine glass properly and how to consume vast quantities of its contents. So quickly it happened.

Before many months had gone by, she woke up in Chicago one gray, Monday morning, in the twelfth story of a hotel. She was in bed with a man she had never seen before. She stepped to the window and jumped.

It happened that the policeman on the beat had known her family for years. When he elbowed his way through the crowd to where her body was lying on the street, he recognized her. He held her head in his hands and he ran his fingers through her hair like he used to do when she was just a little girl. A voice from the crowd said, "How come?"

He looked up through his tears and said, "When you haven't got God, there's nothing to do but jump."

Listen, I believe that. Without Him, we are dead. But with the presence of the Lord Jesus, we live, and there's never a reason to jump.

And I want to invite anyone who will, to come now and give his or her life to Jesus.

[1] *Against Neaera,* quoted, Athenaeus, *Deipnosophistae* 573B.

[2] Juvenal, *Satires* 6.55.

[3] Seneca, *On Benefits* 3.16.1-3

[4] Juvenal, *Satires* 6.308.

[5] Suetonius, *Nero* 28.29.

[6] Serendipity, J. Wallace Hamilton, Fleming H. Revell Co., Westwood, New Jersey, Page 122.

[7] Cyril, J. Davey. Kagawa of Japan. Abingdon Press, New York, 1960, pp. 41-43.

JESUS-MYTH, MAN, OR MESSIAH?

During the days when the West was being settled, many pioneers were making their way over the Oregon trail. On the eastern slopes of the Rockies, they found a streamlet a little too wide to cross in one step. They "two-stepped" across by means of an *ugly lump* protruding from the water in midstream.

As the years passed, other pioneers settled that area, built their cabins, strung fences and tilled fields. One built his cabin close by this streamlet. His door flapped in the wind, but he discovered a *heavy lump* in the middle of the streamlet. He carried it to his front step and it became a door stop.

More years passed. Ribbons of steel spanned the nation, the masses pushed west and modern cities sprang up. A nephew of the old pioneer went east to study geology in a large university. He returned home during vacation. Lo and behold, on the front porch of his uncle's old cabin by the stream he found, not just an *ugly lump,* and not just a *heavy lump* but a *lump of pure gold,* the largest gold nugget ever discovered on the eastern slopes of the Rockies!!! It had been, for three generations, unrecognized as such by the untrained eyes of its handlers.

People look at Jesus Christ in different ways as well. Some give him only a superficial glance. They see *a myth,* an idea that was "a useful aid in the journey of less enlightened men." As one man said to me, "Jesus Christ is a nice idea, but like Santa Claus no one takes him very seriously!"

Others take a more careful look at Jesus, and discover not a myth, but a man. He was a real character in ancient history. Maybe a good man, but *just a man!*

Others who take time to look more carefully at Jesus Christ see *not a myth,* and *not just a man,* but they actually see him to be the Son of God, the Savior of the world, the Lord of life and the only hope there is of making sense of our tangled human situation.

WHAT DO YOU SEE?

When you look at Jesus Christ, what do you see? Many might say, "Obviously, we see the latter or we wouldn't be here." I'm not really convinced that this is always the case. In some areas it's a cultural imperative that people go to church, and it's widely accepted that "good folks believe in Jesus Christ." There is little room among family and friends to acknowledge honest doubts.

So, I believe it's a legitimate and vital question. It's a fundamental question because Jesus himself was concerned about this question.

He said, "Who do men say that the Son of Man is."[1]

He asked his disciples, "What do you think of the Christ? Whose son is he?"[2]

That is the key question.

In fact there are only two big questions! The first one, *"Who is Jesus?"* And if we answer that one validly, the only other question that matters is, *"What does He want from me?"* So I really want us to take this discussion personally because *it really matters what you* think about Jesus Christ.

Let's explore attitudes toward Jesus from the framework of these three ideas: the myth, the man, and God come in the flesh.

JESUS, THE MYTH

It's rather bewildering to me that a number of reasonably well-educated people actually are not convinced Jesus ever really lived. They think of him as "just a Christian myth." (A nice idea that nobody takes very seriously, like Santa Claus.) Some who regularly sit on Sunday pews have real questions about that. This is astounding in the face of available evidence. But, because I know some have doubts, let's explore some of the information.

WITNESSES FROM HISTORY

Pretend that we are in a court of law. We're hearing witnesses to the validity of Jesus. First we'll call the historians. Roman history at the time of Jesus, is sprinkled with ample testimony. In my study is a translation of an exchange of letters between Pliny and Trajan. Trajan was an emperor of Rome. Under the leadership of Trajan severe persecution broke out against the early Christians. Pliny was the governor of a minor province of Rome called Bithynia. Pliny had heard that something was supposed to happen to the Christians, but being way out in the "boondocks," he needed further instructions. So he wrote Trajan to learn just exactly how he was to deal with what he and Trajan both called the "followers of that Galilean."[3] They affirm that Jesus lived. They called him "that Galilean." Though they didn't like the way the people honored him over the emperor of Rome, they still attest to the fact that Jesus lived.

Later, there was a Roman historian by the name of Tacitus who was a contemporary of Jesus. Tacitus declares that Jesus was put to death "under the reign of Tiberius Caesar."[4] This would agree with *Luke 3:1* which states Jesus was baptized in the fifteenth year of the reign of Tiberius Caesar. Even though these people weren't at all friendly to Jesus, they establish his historicity.

Moving to the Jewish historians, we call another witness. When Jewish historians, contemporary to Jesus, are mentioned, it's natural that Flavius Josephus will come first to mind. I suppose half the people here have read some of *The Life and Works of Flavius Josephus.*

Flavius Josephus was a Jew who never did embrace Christianity. Yet he says, "Now there was about this time

Jesus, a wise man." Then he adds, "If it be lawful to call him a man."[5]

Not only does he affirm that Jesus lived then, but that He was such an outstanding character Josephus himself seems unsure that He was "just a man". Flavius Josephus would be approximately thirty years younger than Jesus.

Other groups of historians were actually a part of the early church who drifted away and began counter movements. We usually think of denominational division in Christianity as being a reasonably recent development, but there were some very early splinter groups. The leader of one of these groups was a man by the name of Cerinthus.

Now Cerinthus believed that matter was inherently evil. Therefore, Jesus could never have become a flesh and blood body because God would not touch matter. So he attempted to explain Jesus in another way. Some of the followers of Cerinthus said that if you were to touch the body of Jesus you would not feel anything because he was just an apparition. And others said, "No, he really was physical, but into His physical body, the spirit of God came at His baptism." Others said that when this *man* named Jesus was being crucified on Calvary, the real Jesus who was not a flesh and blood man was standing on the hill watching the execution take place. Cerinthus did a lot of writing. He repeatedly refers to Jesus, the man from Nazareth, and so confirms that Jesus really lived.[6]

History has more, much more, but possibly we could sum it up in the words of Albert Schweitzer in his book entitled, *The Quest of the Historical Jesus.* Schweitzer, of course, is that well-known missionary who died a few years ago. He is supposed to have had three Ph.D.'s before he was thirty years old—one in medicine, one in music and one in religion. After he had tallied up all of the historical evidence for the man, Jesus, he said,

"It must be admitted that there are few characters of

antiquity about whom we possess so much indubitably historical information, of whom we have so many authentic
discourses. The position is much more favourable, for
instance, than in the case of Socrates; for he is pictured to
us by literary men who exercised their creative ability upon
the portrait. Jesus stands much more immediately before
us, because He was depicted by simple Christians without
literary gift."[7]

WITNESSES FROM SCRIPTURE

There is another group of witnesses upon which I will
call. These are the actual writers of the New Testament itself.
Immediately something in you may object. "They don't have
a great deal of credibility to me, because obviously, they
were *trying* to make people believe that Jesus really lived. To
quote them is to beg the question."

Keep in mind that Matthew, Mark, Luke, and John, the
men who wrote the gospels, were Jesus' contemporaries.
Their audience was also made up of Jesus' contemporaries,
some of whom were his neighbors. Now if I had been writing
a spurious document in an attempt to produce faith in some
mythological, non-existent person, I would be very careful. I
would studiously avoid anything that could be checked out. I
would be vague. I certainly would not use places, dates,
events and names.

But the writers of the gospels did not approach things
that way. They appear to expect people would be checking
out their story. And they flung down information as much as
to say, "Here are the facts. You go check. We invite investi-
gation." For example, look at *Luke 1:26.* (This was before
Jesus was born.) The writer says,

> "In the sixth month the angel Gabriel was sent from God to
> a city of Galilee named Nazareth, to a virgin betrothed to a
> man whose name was Joseph, of the house of David; and
> the virgin's name was Mary."

So it lists even the angel's name, the month of the pregnancy,
the woman's name, the man's name, the man's tribe, the

province and the city. All those facts are there!

After Jesus has already begun his personal ministry, in *Matthew 13:54ff* the record says,

> "And coming to his own country he taught them in their synagogue, so that they were astonished, and said, 'Where did this man get this wisdom and these mighty works? Is not this the carpenter's son? Is not his mother called Mary? And are not his brothers James and Joseph and Simon and Judas? And are not all his sisters with us?'"

As much as to say, "All right, check! Go knock on the door and say, 'Hey, do you know if there is a guy in this town named Joseph?'

'Yeah, he's got a carpenter shop down the street.'

'What is his wife's name?'

'Mary.'

'Did he have any children?'

'Yeah, James, Joseph, Simon, Judas, Jesus and some girls.'"

All you had to do was go check the facts and see whether or not this character was real. And yet these writers deliberately supply abundant specific information. In fact, it has become almost ludicrous when you come to *Luke 3:1.* Almost as if Luke were taunting the skeptics:

> "In the fifteenth year of the reign of Tiberius Caesar, Pontius Pilate being governor of Judea, and Herod being tetrarch of Galilee, and his brother Philip tetrarch of the region of Ituraea and Trachonitis, and Lysanias tetrarch of Abilene, in the high-priesthood of Annas and Caiaphas, the word of God came to John the son of Zechariah in the wilderness ... "

Almost as if Luke is saying, "Hey, if you are still suspicious, look at *all these facts."*

Later in that chapter there is more. We not only know who Jesus was, we know where he walked and slept, where he ate, his friends, his enemies, what made him angry, what made him happy. We know his father's name, his grandfather's name, his greatgrandfather's name. He was,

"Jesus, the son of Joseph, the son of Heli, the son of Matthat, the son of Levi, the son of Melchi, the son of Jannai, the son of Joseph, the son of Mattathias, the son of Amos, the son of Nahum, the son of Esli, the son of Naggai, the son of Maath, the son of Mattathias, the son of Semein, the son of Josech, the son of Joda, the son of Joanan, the son of Rhesa, the son of Zerubbabel, the son of Shealtiel, the son of Neri, the son of Melchi, the son of Addi, the son of Cosam, the son of Elmadam, the son of Er, the son of Joshua, the son of Eliezer, the son of Jorim, the son of Matthat, the son of Levi, the son of Simeon, the son of Judah, the son of Joseph, the son of Jonam, the son of Eliakim, the son of Melea, the son of Menna, the son of Mattatha, the son of Nathan, the son of David, the son of Jesse, the son of Obed, the son of Boaz, the son of Sala, the son of Nahshon, the son of Amminadab, the son of Admin, the son of Arni, the son of Hezron, the son of Perez, the son of Judah, the son of Jacob, the son of Isaac, the son of Abraham, the son of Terah, the son of Nahor, the son of Serug, the son of Reu, the son of Peleg, the son of Eber, the son of Shelah, the son of Cainan, the son of Arphaxad, the son of Shem, the son of Noah, the son of Lamech, the son of Methuselah, the son of Enoch, the son of Jared, the son of Mahalaleel, the son of Cainan, the son of Enos, the son of Seth, the son of Adam, *the son of God.*[8]

Now! Really! Would someone care to rise and recite the genealogies of Santa Claus? The person who argues that the man, Jesus, never really lived either denies the facts or is not familiar with them!

JESUS, THE MAN

Most people acknowledge that the man, Jesus, lived. The question is, "What about this man? Was he anything m than just an unusual man?" A large constituency today declares, "No! He was a great man, but he was *just a man.*"

Some regard him as an unusually wise philosopher. Presumbly there are some senses in which one might refer to Jesus as a philosopher. A philosopher has some ideas about the meaning of life, and Jesus definitely had ideas about life! But, the word philosopher actually comes from two different Greek words, *"phileo,"* i. e. love, and *"sophia,"* i. e. wisdom. A "lover of wisdom" to the Greeks, which was understood as a "seeker after truth." By *that* definition, Jesus never was a philosopher. He was not seeking for the truth. He *was the embodiment of truth.* He was God's truth broken into space and time in visible human form. And that is why he said, "I am the way, and the truth, and the life; no one comes to the Father, but by me."[9]

"I am the bread of life; he who comes to me shall not hunger, and he who believes in me shall never thirst."[10]

"I am the light of the world; he who follows me will not walk in darkness, but will have the light of life."[11]

"I am the resurrection and the life; he who believes in me, though he die, yet shall he live."[12]

Jesus is saying, *"I'm* not looking for something. I'm what *you* are looking for, the way and the truth and the life."

Jesus sometimes is lumped in with the ancient, oft quoted philosophers, Socrates, Plato, Aristotle. Socrates had some good ideas about life, but Socrates committed suicide. Plato was a wise man and still affects our thinking today, but Plato was a practicing homosexual. Aristotle probably influenced our thinking more than any of the ancient philosophers. Our system of logic is built on his thinking, (and some of our theology, I'm afraid). But Aristotle died in drunken debauchery. They somehow could not get their lives to validate their philosophies.

Jesus *was* what he taught. He validated everything He said by living it out. It was so compellingly beautiful that the people were drawn as to a magnet. So demanding, that multitudes also "turned away."

Otis Gatewood tells of an incident that occurred in Frankfurt, Germany soon after World War II. He and some other Americans were teaching the gospel among students at the University of Frankfurt. One of the girls befriended an Oriental girl who was Islamic. She tried to convert this girl to Jesus. They debated whether the Bible was better attested than the Koran, whether the ethics of Jesus were superior to those of Mohammed, and other areas of comparative religion. But they seemed to make no progress. The girl came to Brother Gatewood and said, "I really need some help. I have said everything I know to this girl and not only am I not getting anywhere, I think she is about to convert me to Islam. Help!"

So Brother Gatewood replied, "Did you ever just tell her about Jesus?"

"Well, that's what we have been talking about."

"No, did you ever tell her about the man Jesus, what he was really like. Not the arguments he used on the scribes and Pharisees or whatever, but *what He was like.*"

"Digest the gospels," he said. "They tell the story of Jesus. Then go tell the girl what you've found."

She nearly flunked some courses trying to get Jesus in her mind. But after she had digested thoroughly enough so that she felt at home with the narrative and "knew the person," she called the Oriental girl in.

"We'll just talk one more time," she said. "It will take a long time, but when we are finished, if we have not gotten anywhere, we will drop it." So they sat down and shared Jesus. She became so absorbed that she did not even notice how the Islamic girl was being affected.

When she paused for breath at the end of her story, the Oriental girl was crying.

"What's wrong?" she asked.

The Oriental girl said, "Well, why didn't you tell me this before? We don't have anyone like that in Islam. I want to be a Christian. I want to be like Him. Just tell me how to get started." Jesus doesn't need defense. He needs proclamation!

There is something different about Jesus. That is why it is said, "He taught them as one who had authority, and not as the scribes."[13] That authority does not mean he swung a big stick and said, "You better listen to me." It means he was not quoting some wise and learned man. *He* was the authority. "Here is the way it is." And there was something about the way He said it that was irresistible. His words were also authenticated by His life. He is so much more than mere man. Paul makes that so clear.

> "If Christ has not been raised, your faith is futile and you
> are still in your sins. Then those also who have fallen asleep
> in Christ have perished. If for this life only we have hoped
> in Christ, we are of all men most to be pitied."[14]

In other words, if we just see Jesus as another wise man, why should we believe what he says? There are many wise men. But few agree together.

JESUS AS SAVIOR AND LORD

Everyone is looking for a solid place to let his weight down. Thousands feel, "If I only knew for sure what is right and could not be wrong, I would be willing to give my whole life to it. But, I don't know what is valuable. I have tried this idea and I have tried that. Each seemed pretty good for awhile, and then I find something doesn't fit. One man seems wise until I find another wise man who differs with

That is Jesus' message. I by myself am lost. We know we are guilty! How often do you find yourself rationalizing, yeilding to the temptation to do something you know could jeopardize your happiness? How often do you risk someone else's happiness? All of us at times feel bound and unclean because of our sins.

The Bible says everyone is a sinner. Bad news! But the good news is not further remorse and self-analysis. It is forgiveness!!! And that forgiveness is available only in Jesus Christ.

John said, "Behold, the lamb of God, who takes away the sin of the world!"[2][3]

We must acknowledge that we are failures and say, "Lord, save me because I believe in you." And He says, "I will, if you will turn *from* yourself *to* me. If you will just declare me before men. If you will just be baptized to join me in my death and resurrection experience, you will be forgiven of your sins—they will be washed away with my blood." Forgiveness![2][4]

JESUS

Walk carefully here. Many people believe He is the Son of God and even want Him to be their Savior. But they want salvation— . . . period! They want a Savior that comes on like Mother after a greasy meal and with spot remover dabs away the problem, leaving us in our dirty clothes with sloppy habits.

But He wants to be both *Savior* and *Lord.* C. S. Lewis said he used to get the toothache sometimes and he knew if he went to his mother she would put aspirins in his tooth to kill the pain. But he would not go to his mother. She would give him an aspirin, all right, but it would not stop there. She would take him to the dentist, and the dentist won't quit till he has filled every tooth in your head. He would rather endure the pain than have that long commitment.

We are like that. If there is something wrong with my personality, I want to get rid of it. It is souring relationships with the people around me. If I could just have that little thing fixed. "Hey, Jesus can fix." So I want Him to fix things up, and then be out of my hair. But that is not the way he operates.

> "If you confess with your lips that *Jesus is Lord* and believe in your heart that God raised him from the dead, you will be saved. For man believes with his heart and so is justified, and he confesses with his lips and so is saved."[25]

There was a time when I asked a baptismal candidate simply, "Do you believe that Jesus is the Son of God?" Now, I also ask, "Do you want Him to be the Lord of your life?" A lord is a controller, a ruler, a governor, an owner. And that means, then, that when I accept Jesus, the Son of God as my Savior and my Lord, every particular of my life is surrendered into His will. I begin to feed on the Bible to find out what God's will is for me. "If you love me, you will keep my commandments."[26] That just follows as the night to day. If the sun comes over the hill, there will be light in the world. "If you love me, you will keep my commandments." That is how we express our love to Jesus.

When Jesus is Lord, every decision I make, from the time I get out of bed in the morning until I pillow my head at night is decided in the climate, "What does the Lord want?"

THE FOUNDATION ISSUE

Let's go back to the beginning of the sermon for just a moment. We read from *Matthew 16*. This took place "in the regions of Caesarea Philippi."

God has a way not only of saying beautiful things, but of putting them in beautiful settings. The city of Caesarea Philippi was not always called Caesarea Philippi. In times shrouded by the mists of remote antiquity it was called Paneas. It was built in honor of a shepherd god, half goat and half man. His name was Pan.

Times changed and Paneas was destroyed. It was considered for centuries to be (in the words of T. B. Larimore), "haunted and inhabited by jackals and bats and hissing serpents but not by the sons and daughters of men."

Much later came a budding young politician. He saw a way to make his political mark. His name was Herod Philip. As a relatively "little shot," it seemed politically helpful to link his name with a "big shot." The big shot he chose was the top cheese of all, Caesar. So he rebuilt this little village and called it "Caesarea Philippi." Caesar-Philip-town. That was a master-stroke of politics. We still remember it, don't we.

The little village of Caesarea Philippi, I'm told by those who have visited there, is built on rocky country. The bedrock is visible under very little topsoil. The area is a massive plain of rock.

When Caesarea Philippi was rebuilt it was surrounded by a wall of solid rock. Even the buildings, not just the walls and the floors, but even the roofs, were made of stone. About a mile toward the "golden gates of the morning" stood rock-ribbed Mt. Hermon. When the sun rose the shadow of Mt. Hermon would fall on Caesarea Philippi.

Up on the shoulder of Mt. Hermon was a little fortress where people could run to hide if they were chased out of Caesarea Philippi. It was also built out of solid rock.

Now it is marvelous that God set this event at this place. He said, "In the regions of Caesarea Philippi, Jesus, (called 'the Rock of Ages,' 'the Rock cleft for sinners'), said to Peter (whose very name meant rock, a little stone), "Who do men say that I, the Son of Man, am?"

Peter said, "Some say you are Moses, some say you are Elijah, some say one of the prophets."

"Who do you say that I am?"

It was then and there in this rock-founded, rock-bounded, rock-builded, rock-surrounded, rock-shadowed, and rock-protected city that Jesus, the *Rock* of Ages spoke solemnly to Peter, a *little* stone, "Peter, you are a little stone, and on this *massive ledge of rock,"* (this confession you have made—as massive and solid as Caesarea Philippi), "on *this rock* I will build my church and the gates of Hell will never prevail against it."² ⁷ That is the solid rock on which all else rests.. If that is not true, nothing matters much. We would all be at sea! But, *He is God.* And that will be true when the world is on fire.

I believe that. I do not think I would live long without believing that. I want you to believe it too. If you will not accept Him, you will be sad as long as you live. But if you genuinely believe Him, let Him take hold of your life as Savior by your confessing Him and being baptized for the remission of your sins, you can go on proclaiming Him as the Lord and controller of your life.

"What *do* you think of Christ?" It *really* does matter what you believe!

---

¹*Matthew 16:13*
²*Matthew 22:42*
³Melmoth, William, "To the Emperor of Trajan," *Pliny Letters,* Book X, Section XCVI, (Cambridge: Harvard University Press, 1963), p. 401-405.

⁵Whiston, William, tr. *The Life and Works of Flavius Josephus,* (New York: Holt, Rinehart and Winston, no date), p. 535.

⁶M'Clintock and Strong, *Cyclopedia of Biblical, Theological, and Ecclesiastical Literature, Vol. II,* p. 190-191.

⁷Schweitzer, Albert, *The Quest of the Historical Jesus,* (New York: The MacMillan Company, 1961), p. 6.

⁸*Luke 3:23-38*
⁹*John 14:6.*
¹⁰*John 6:35.*
¹¹*John 8:12.*
¹²*John 11:25.*
¹³*Mark 1:22.*
¹⁴*I Corinthians 15:17-19.*

[15] *John 20:30-31.*
[16] *John 14:9.*
[17] *John 8:19.*
[18] *Mark 9:37.*
[19] *John 15:23.*
[20] *John 5:23.*
[21] *John 1:1, 14.*
[22] *John 3:19-21.*
[23] *John 1:29.*
[24] *Romans 6:1-4, Galatians 3:26-28, Colossians 2:12, Acts 2:38-39.*
[25] *Romans 10:9-10.*
[26] *John 14:15.*
[27] Personal paraphrase of

OUR UNKNOWN GOD

In every life story there is at least one chapter of wanderlust. Even if our travel dreams never become reality, we make our journeys by books, by movies, and by imagination. You are invited to take a journey with me. We'll pretend that we are boarding an aircraft in New York. In a few hours the broad, green Atlantic is beneath us.

The scene and the direction change. Now we are over land again. Then the sparkling blue waters of the Mediterranean are in view. We begin our descent into the ancient city of Athens. After the plane touches the runway, we emerge into a strange kind of world. Around us are marvelous contrasts. Adjacent to buildings constructed this year are other buildings which have been standing since long before Jesus walked the earth.

In the center of the city we see steep, dramatic hills at the top of which are the ruins of stately buildings. We make our way up the hill. It isn't long until we have come over the stone steps to the ancient ruins, the Areopagus. Could it be our feet are on the very spot which Paul once stood so many years ago?

In the first century, too, Athens was a busy city. People came from all over, the Bible says, "To hear or to tell some new thing." Possibly the atmosphere was akin to the courthouse square of a busy little county seat, where the fellows play checkers, swap lies and spit and whittle. It was a place where new thoughts and old thoughts were shared.

Then Paul spoke:

"Men of Athens, I perceive that in every way you are very religious. For as I passed along, and observed the objects of your worship, I found also an altar with this inscription, 'To an unknown god.' What therefore you worship as unknown, this I proclaim to you. The God who made the world and everything in it, being Lord of heaven and earth, does not live in shrines made by man, nor is he served by human hands, as though he needed anything, since he himself gives to all men life and breath and everything. And he made from one every nation of men to live on all the face of the earth, having determined allotted periods and the boundaries of their habitiation, that they should seek God, in the hope that they might feel after him and find him. Yet he is not far from each one of us, for, 'In him we live and move and have our being'; as even some of your poets have said, 'For we are indeed his offspring.' Being then God's offspring, we ought not to think that the Deity is like gold, or silver, or stone, a representation by the art and imagination of man. The times of ignorance God overlooked, but now he commands all men everywhere to repent, because he has fixed a day on which he will judge the world in righteousness by a man whom he has appointed and of this he has given assurance to all men by raising him from the dead."

"Now when they heard of the resurrection of the dead, some mocked; but others said, 'We will hear you again about this.'"[1]

This was Paul's approach to the hearts of those in Athens. Though twenty centuries have come and gone since that time, I think the apostle's message would be similar if he were speaking to us. He may still borrow the same text from the altar, directed "to the unknown God."

In spite of the fact that we talk of God, have learned some of His laws, go through a weekly ritual in honor of God, for many of us there is a real sense in which God is a stranger. We see Him as "totally other" or an "unseen power." We have little personal acquaintance with "Our Father."

A story is told that some years ago a young man grew up in the Ozarks. He went away to seek his fortune in the wide, wicked world, and became a famous actor. He returned to the long, blue shadow of the tall, green Ozarks to visit.

The village was gathered at an old time song fest. They wanted him to get up and say a few words to display his art. In fact, he was asked to quote the familiar 23rd Psalm.

After some persuasion he agreed on one condition. There was an old man present. If Farmer Brown would get up and recite the 23rd Psalm after the actor, he would consent. Some folks thought he was trying to humiliate Farmer Brown, but the actor had something in mind.

His diction was marvelous, the resonance of his voice absolutely spellbound the people, and every gesture was fitted to the words. When he had finished, the audience sat in rapt attention. Then Farmer Brown got up. Of course, he was nervous. His voice was dry. He didn't know how to pronounce some of the words properly. But he began with a fire in his soul and with a spark in his eye. He said, "The *Lord* is *my* shepherd; *I* shall not want . . . "

By the time he had finished quoting the 23rd Psalm, many of the people were on the verge of tears. Children in the audience said, "What made the difference?" The actor replied, "It is clear. I know the *Psalm,* but Farmer Brown knows the *shepherd."*

We know about the Psalm, we can quote the passages, we have some idea of organized religion, but the hungry heart of man will not be satisfied merely with a larger dose of organized religion. Do we "know the shepherd?" Something in man is only fulfilled by communion with God.

THREE QUESTIONS

Three questions about God: Not the questions children ask, like, "Where does God live?" and "Who is God's grandmother?" and "Does God have a pet cat?" or "Who is God's wife?" But, we ask three questions of importance to mature minds.

"Is there really a God?" "What is God made out of?" "Does God have a personality?"

IS THERE A GOD?

That first question: About fifteen years ago a poll was taken in this country to find out how many people believed in God. Ninety-seven percent said that they believed there was a God of some sort. Two percent of the people said that they didn't believe in God, and one percent said they didn't know! I know of no recent poll. But, I would be surprised if the number who say they believe would be as large.

Is there really a God? George Gallup doesn't settle such questions. Likely most of you would indicate you believe by your very presence here. Yet, sometimes we say we believe in God, simply because it seems like a comfortable thing to do. The people we respect seem to believe that! Whenever a doubt comes to mind, rather than confront it and honestly deal with it, it's easier to brush it under the rug. That works fine as long as there are lots of Christians around and everything is going good. But when the pressure comes and one is alone with his doubts, that kind of faith lacks substance.

There are some *reasons to believe* in God. Most doubters cannot be argued into accepting the idea that God lives. If someone is of a disposition not to believe in God, all of the argument in the world will not change his mind. Rather, evangelism today should seek to lead people to *want* to believe in God. I frankly confess that one of the main reasons that I believe in God is because *I want to.* Trying to persuade someone by argument to believe in God is like trying to persuade someone that the rainbow is beautiful when he will not open his eyes and look at it, or that a rose has a lovely fragrance when he will not smell it. Until he is willing to look and smell, he doesn't know of the loveliness. When he is ready, there is no need to persuade him. The rainbow and the rose are self-validating. So is God.

However, there are some real reasons to believe in God.

Faith is not irrational. In the *first place,* I believe in God because of things *outside* of me, and *secondly,* because of things *inside* of me.

EVIDENCE OUTSIDE ME

Let's look outside for awhile. Anyone who has spent much time with a microscope has spent time in awe at that tiny, little world invisible to the naked eye. One drop of water is full of all sorts of beautiful, colorful, living things with marvelous harmony and design about them. Even the germs that make us sick look pretty under a microscope. Naturally one wonders, "Who designed these tiny worlds?"

Now to the telescope: Look into the heavens at night as myriads and heavenly bodies are whirling in space with mathematical precision as they have been doing for centuries. Something inside of me says, "How big is space? And if we could travel to the farthest star and with the world's most powerful telescope look again into space and discover that there are only millions more stars, where would it end? *Is* there an end?" Finally imagination is exhausted so it builds a fence, but beyond the fence would still be more.

This means we can actually *see* into eternity. Do you have difficulty grasping the idea that God *always* was and always *will be?* Eternity! Try then to grasp how far it is to the other side of the universe. If the eye can "see" infinity, the "mind' can conceive of eternity. It takes little wisdom to begin to ask, "How did it come to be?" "Why the design; why the marvelous harmony?"

Strip away the tools of science and look with the naked eye at what God places in front of us every day. Or listen to the roar of a waterfall, the babbling of a brook, the song of a bird in the morning or the night wind through the trees. See ten thousand flowers flung across ten thousand hills. Watch the grasses springing from the silent, sleeping sod of the springtime and you will see the footprints of God. His love and artistry are in the rainbow, the sunset and a simple cloud against the blue sky.

> O Lord my God! When I in awesome wonder
> Consider all the worlds Thy hands have made,
> I see the stars, I hear the rolling thunder,
> Thy pow'r throughout the universe displayed,
>
> Then sings my soul, my Saviour God to Thee;
> How great Thou art, how great Thou art![2]

That's what the Psalmist was saying in the 19th Psalm: "The Heavens declare the glory of God and the earth shows His handiwork."

EVIDENCE INSIDE ME

But now let's look inside of ourselves awhile. There's something so obvious it's significance is easily overlooked. Through history, where there were *men,* you will also find *gods.* There is something in the very nature of a man that cannot bear a vacant Heaven.

Why? One may explain it this way. "Well, it rose out of our basic insecurity; we had to invent the idea of a god because we just couldn't answer all of the questions by ourselves." Man's need created God.

But could the reverse be true? Imagine a little four-year-old child, wandering lost through the aisles of a large department store. He's crying. "What's wrong, son?" you ask.

He answers, "I want my mommy."

Do you sit down and say, "Listen, son, you don't have a mommy. You just feel lonely and insecure, so you invented the idea of a mommy in the hopes that you might find some security."

No! The reason he is lonely and insecure is because he *has* a mother. Not vice-versa! And the reason there is a big hole in my reality until I discover a relationship with the creator of the universe is because *there is a creator of the universe.* As surely as male and female long for each other, humankind and Godkind long for each other.

"Well," you may say, "that doesn't seem very solid. You are basing your faith on an inborn instinct."

I like to hunt. Until a few years ago, I don't know how many hundreds of miles I walked, year after year, every fall up in British Columbia, hunting deer. Sometimes, a deer would be walking through the forest. I would think, "Soon as he emerges from behind that birch tree—bango!" But more than once a deer would sense my presence and run directly away from me behind the cover of a tree trunk scarce ten inches thick. How did he know I was there? How did he know exactly what angle to run?

God built an instinct into him. His life depends on it.

The wild geese nest in the area where we lived in Canada. The people who band those geese and study their migration have discovered they will fly thousands of miles, yet return to nest in the same pond where they were hatched! Across all of those thousands of miles, how do they find that exact spot? There is something built in. A God-given sense—an instinct for survival.

The salmon spawn in the rivers where we lived. They go down through the little streamlets, into the rivers, into the bigger rivers and finally are lost in the vast depth of the ocean. When they are ready to spawn they return up the rivers, back to the little, tiny streamlet where they were hatched! How come?

I believe God gave more sense to us that He gave to a fish or a deer or a goose. I believe the instinct that is written into the nature of man does mean something. I have a "God-shaped vacuum" in my heart. My life depends upon it. I hunger for God precisely *because* there *is* a God. It is reasonable to believe.

I need not persuade you. If your faith is weak, but your soul is hungry you are looking for reasons to believe. On the other hand, if you are in rebellion against God, and don't want to believe (even subconsciously), you probably would not accept the most convincing reasons.

Finally in this connection, one of the happiest things about accepting a relationship with the living God is that *you need not fear you are wrong.* Once after I had said that, a high school girl said, "'You seem rather egotistical. Do you think there's no possibility you are wrong?"

"Yes," I said, "There's a possibility I'm wrong. I don't think I am, but there is a possibility I am. However, *if* I am, I'm not afraid."

She had told me she didn't believe in God, so I said, "Aren't you afraid you might be wrong? You see, if I'm wrong, I haven't lost anything. I've lived a happy life. Life has made sense to me. My days are full and my nights peaceful. When they carry me out to the cemetery and put me in the hole in the ground, I will have had a good life, *even if I'm wrong.*"

"But now, if you discover you are wrong, when they carry you to a cemetery, it will be a different story, won't it? You will have forever to regret it!"

WHAT IS GOD MADE OF?

The second question is, *"What is God made of?"* I suppose we don't know the answer because we don't understand totally what *spirit* is. *John 4:24* says, "God is spirit."

The King James version says, "God is *a* spirit." That makes it sound like he's one among a host of ghosts. But the original really says, "God is spirit."

But now, what *is* he made of; what does that mean? The Bible says in Deut. 6:4, "Hear, O Israel, the Lord our God is one god." Yet, the Bible confuses the issue, saying that *one* God, is made up of three manifestations, three personalities, three persons. (I don't know what to call them.)

One of these "entities," (which we choose to call "persons,") these manifestations of God, is God the *Father*. In Genesis the first chapter the Bible says, *"God* created the heavens and the earth." The word "God" is plural. Then God said, "Let *us* make man in our own image." With whom is he talking? Who is the other agent in creation? *John 1:1* tells us that *Jesus* created the earth. *Genesis 1:1* says *God* created the earth. What is this plurality?

Moving to *Matthew chapter three,* at the baptism of Jesus, we see the plurality delineated. Jesus is being baptized in the River Jordan by John. The voice of the Father from Heaven is saying, "This is my beloved son, in whom I am well pleased. Hear him." Between them is the Holy Spirit descending in a form as of a dove. Three "persons." The Father, the Son and the Holy Spirit.

That is why the Bible tells us to "Go therefore and make disciples of all nations, baptizing them into the name of the Father, and of the Son and of the Holy Spirit." *(Matthew 28:19.)*

The *Father* is called God. "To us there is one God, the Father of whom are all things. *(I Cor. 8:6)* the *Son* is called God. "In the beginning was the Word, and the Word was with God, and the Word was God." *(John 1:1)* "The Word became flesh and dwelt among us." (v. 14) The *Holy Spirit* is called God. Ananias had lied about the price of his property. Peter said to him, "Why has Satan filled your heart to lie to the *Holy Spirit . . .?* You have not lied unto men, but unto *God."* *(Acts 5:3-4).* So the Father, the Son and the Holy Spirit are all called God, and yet they are even geographically separated for us at the baptism of Jesus.

I don't understand this, but I believe it. (I don't know how electricity works either, but I believe it.)

God is three and God is one. All three of these "persons" of God are active. When the world was created; God, the Father, created; God, the Son, created; and Job says the Spirit was active in creating the world.

The more important fact is that God the Father was active in creating His body, the church, the new humanity. It was in His mind before the foundation of the world. *(Eph. 3:11)* Jesus said, *"I will build my church." (Matt. 16:18)* The Holy Spirit was active in the creation of the church. Jesus said he would send His Holy Spirit who would guide the apostles "into all truth and they would not speak from themselves, but whatever they would hear, that would they speak." And the Holy Spirit would "show them the things that were to come." *(Jno. 16:13)* The apostles gave the message of the early church. The Holy Spirit was present on the Day of Pentecost when the power was given to the early church, and the Holy Spirit is present in the life of a Christian when he becomes a part of the church.

> "Do you not know that your body is a temple of the Holy Spirit within you, which you have from God? You are not your own; you were bought with a price. So glorify God in your body." *(I Cor. 6:19-20)*

Father, Son, and Holy Spirit, all are active in the creation of the church.

DOES GOD HAVE A PERSONALITY?

Now, let's turn from the technical to that third question. I like it best because it's warmer. *"Does God have a personality?"*

It may seem irreverent to refer to the nature of God as His "personality" since we customarily evaluate personality in human characteristics. We speak of "lousy personalities" and so forth. But, there may be a real sense in which God has · personality. Only two facets of his infinitely many-sided personality are of interest to us just here.

Our God should never be regarded as some benign, old, simple-minded grandfather with sentimental feelings about everybody, as if it doesn't matter to Him what goes on in His universe. The God of the Bible has real firmness and strength of character with definite ideas as to what He wants. In fact, when the Ten Commandments are declared in *Exod. 20:5* it says:

> " . . . for I the Lord your God am a jealous God, visiting the iniquity of the fathers upon the children to the third and the fourth generation of those who hate me, but showing steadfast love to thousands of those who love me and keep my commandments."

God is a jealous God! When God's will is thwarted; when God's designs are disregarded, chaos results in the universe. The life of the one who is out of harmony with the will of God is deeply unfulfilling, at best. Nothing fits.

When the fathers disregard God, this spills over into the lives of the children, often to the third and the fourth generation. Not that the children are guilty of the father's sins, but they often inherit the father's lifestyle and value system.

"God visits those iniquities. to the third and fourth generation. Similar sentiments are stated in the New Testament.

> " . . . and to grant rest with us to you who are afflicted, when the Lord Jesus is revealed from heaven with his mighty angels in flaming fire, inflicting vengeance upon those who do not know God and upon those who do not obey the gospel of our Lord Jesus. They shall suffer the punishment of eternal destruction and exclusion from the presence of the Lord and from the glory of his might." *(II Thess. 1:7-9)*

God will one day judge those who are in rebellion against Him. *God is a god of judgement.* "It is a fearful thing to fall into the hands of the living God," says the writer to the Hebrews.

"But as·for the cowardly, the faithless, the polluted, as for murderers, fornicators, sorcerers, idolaters, and all liars, their lot shall be in the lake that burns with fire and sulphur, which is the second death." *(Rev. 21:8)*

The consequences of rebellion toward God not only result in disharmony in this life, but there are *eternal implications.* God is a righteous God who cannot tolerate rebellion and sin in his presence.

THE LOVING FATHER

But, we cannot end the sermon there. No one is saved by the wrath of God. He is saved by the mercy of God and the grace of God. "He who does not love does not know God; for God is love." *(I Jno. 4:8)* "The Lord is not slow about his promise as some count slowness, but is forbearing toward you, not wishing that any should perish, but that all should reach repentance." *(II Pet. 3:9)* And in the well-known words, "God so loved the world that He gave His only Son, that whoever believes in him should not perish but have eternal life. For God sent the Son into the world, not to condemn the world, but that the world might be saved through Him." *(Jno. 3:16)* This is the personality of God. I believe with all of my heart that the message for which the world hungers is the love of God and the mercy of God.

We cannot totally separate God's love from God's wrath, because one of the ways he manifests His love is to declare His wrath against everything that's destructive to well-being, and to righteousness and to good. Yet, God's love so infinitely surpasses description. Is there anything more powerful that one could ever do in another's life, than to convincingly and with such force and power that it comes through with a ring of truth, tell them that God loves them?

It startles a clerk in the store when she makes your change if (with prayer in your heart and by the Spirit of God) you look into his or her eyes and say, "God loves you. He has a great plan for your life, did you know that?" That's a powerful concept.

One of the reasons that Christians have such listless impact on the world today is because we hear that, but *don't* hear it. A boy was telling me about his church-going experience. He was a good church-goer. He could stand up; sit down, bow, lift up his eyes, drop in the money, drink the cup, you know, do everything at the right time. But, it never came through to him what was happening till one evening they were praying at the end of the service. It suddenly dawned on him, "Hey, we're talking to God!" He got so excited with it he forgot himself and grabbed the guy next to him *right in the middle of the prayer* and said, "Hey, you know what we're doing? We're actually talking to *God!*" Of course, everybody around him thought he had lost his marbles. But it was a moment of insight for him!

If we can *just realize that God loves us!!* If I made a million dollars an hour for the rest of my life, I couldn't pay for the meaning to me, in my own life, when I discovered that God loved *me,* Lynn Anderson, and knew that I didn't need to be lost!!! Inspite of my sins, *He* loved *me* that much. Praise His Name!

All Bible doctrine is, in one way or another, tied into the love of God. If we cut doctrine loose from love it is powerless and can help no one. It is like cutting the crop when it is still young and green, before the grain comes out. There is nothing to harvest. There is no life in it.

If we feed doctrine to the world, doctrine which does not flow out of the love of God and reflect the love of God, we feed them on *husks.* They will starve. Such a message will have little appeal to the hungry searcher.

In evangelistic meetings I usually spend at least the first few nights trying to convince folks that God loves them and *they can* be saved. Once, about the third night, a brother approached me in the foyer.

"Listen," he said, "I appreciate your talks, but when are you going to start preaching the gospel?"

Mischievously, I played innocent. "What do you mean?"

He wanted me to hammer away on his pet themes and his favorite doctrinal points. That would make him feel comfortable. It would confirm the fact that he was all right, and everybody else was wrong.

My heart went out to him, not that the things that he believed in were not important, but that he was clinging to a hull. The joy that comes from proclaiming the gospel ought to be the joy of good news. Doctrine by itself is so dead and empty and lifeless. It's only when God's love enters someone's heart and breaks down his resistance that he becomes responsive to the Father. Then doctrinal compliance will follow with joy and he can rightly relate to God.

How do we describe the love of God? Dare we try? One poet did!

> Could I with ink the oceans fill
> And were the earth of parchment made
> And every blade of grass a quill
> And every man a scribe by trade
> To write the love of God above
> Would drain the ocean dry
> And the scroll would not contain
> The whole, though stretched from sky to sky.

All this poet really said was, "I don't know how to say it." Every feeble attempt I've ever made to speak of God's love seems so insipid, so bland. The mystery is so much for me, I'd rather just *think* about it.

Can we compare His love to other kinds of love? For example, animal love:

The eagle loves it's young. A naturalist watched eagles while a forest fire swept toward their nest. The nest was on a pinnacle of rock. There were pine trees all around it. As the garlands of purple and blue smoke began to weave themselves around that nest, the mother flapped her wings trying to push her little ones off, as if she would give them a crash course in flying. They couldn't fly, so she stayed and screamed at the fire, making threatening motions toward it. Finally she simply spread her wings over the little ones in the nest and perished with her eaglets in the flames.

That is poignantly beautiful. But it really doesn't compare with God's love.

Possibly we could make comparisons with the human mother's love for her children.

A dear friend of mine tells of his grandmother's withered hand. No one ever said much about it, but all of the family somehow reverenced that hand. He asked his mother about it. She told that when his mother and her family were all little children they lived in an old house. That was back in the days when women had ten children instead of two with no electric dishwashers and gadgets to help do the work.

They had a wood stove. One leg of the stove was propped up with a block. The stove was glowing red-hot. The children were playing with a ball which got away from them and rolled under the stove. Quick as a flash one of the little ones went under the stove after it. The block was bumped and the stove began to fall. Jay's grandmother took hold of the red-hot stove with her hand and held it until someone could retrieve the child. Her flesh actually burned to the bone, crippling her hand for life. But that hand was almost sacred in that family. Why? Obviously because it was an eloquent symbol of her love for them.

Still somehow, that doesn't really get us into God's love. His love is of infinitely large dimensions. A glimpse of God's love is shown us when we look at the cross of Jesus Christ.

To adequately appreciate what the cross means we must first view the black background on which its glory is painted.

Before the cross are long centuries when humankind was locked up in the prison house of sin awaiting the day of execution, and someone had thrown away the key. Man was wrapped in the slimy coils of the serpent with no one to extricate him. Over the hills and into the distant past streamed long lines of stumbling, heartbroken pilgrims. Some paused at intervals to place a loved one in a grave. They wept with a sorrow that said, "I will never see you again." For them the end of life was only a hole in the ground!

Ah, but look. Against that background, like the rising of the morning sun, dawns the *cross of Jesus Christ.* You see, God loved us "while we were still sinners."

If you had been present when Jesus was crucified, could you have seen the love of God?

"No," you say, "I don't see how it was God who showed love when He let someone else do His dying for Him."

But, you see, God was the one on the cross. The crucified one was the *son* of the Father.

Can you imagine a four-star general with ranks of soldiers stretched out to the right and left who loves his child? Can he watch while some terrible monster tears his child to pieces in his very presence? Is that the dreadful scene you see the night Jesus was in Gethsemane as God was watching.

If you will allow human characteristics to God for a moment, see Him in heaven with long ranks of angels on every hand. With a nod of His head he could send a heavenly detatchment that could wipe the world out of existence, let alone rescue His son.

Now look at Gethsemane. The smell of death is in the place. The shadow of the cross has fallen across the garden, and across the pained eyes of Jesus. A cry rises through the darkness, all the way to glory, to the ears of the Father.

"Father, if it's possible, let this cup pass from me." In human feeling that translates, "Don't let me go to the cross if there is another way."

In heaven do you hear the angels cease their singing and draw themselves to attention. Again the cry, "Father, if it's possible let . . . " Can you see the great chest heave and the heavenly chin quiver and the tears of God begin to roll. Even a third time!

Why doesn't He do something? Why doesn't He rescue His Son. He will be destroyed!

The Father could see His son, but He could also see me, and He could see you. He could see those long lines of helpless ones back over the rim of history and He could hear their sobbing and ours. What's more, He *loved us.* Can we restrain a whispered, "Hallelujah! He loves us!" He sent an angel to His son. "It must be done this way." And the God of Heaven stood and watched and anguished while they killed Jesus because *He loves me.* Just because He loves me. That's my God. What a "personality"!

TO SPURN LOVE?

Some years ago in a state not too far removed from this one, a young boy was ready to finish high school. His parents always wanted him to go to college. Then his father died rather suddenly, leaving no estate, no insurance and no money. His mother wanted to fulfill the dream she and her husband had for their boy. She worked in the fields in the summer. She chopped cotton in the early year and in the late fall she would be dragging a long sack, pulling cotton, her fingers blue with the cold.

In the winter she would scrub floors, take in ironing or do sewing. A year went by and she got him into college. Another year passed and her clothes were threadbare and her back stooped a little and the furrows in her cheeks were a little deeper. The sparkle in her eye remained though, as she kept on working, working, working.

Finally the day of graduation came. Her son stood with all of the graduates, proudly decked in cap and gown. He looked out over the audience. He saw parents of his classmates. There was a man with an expensive-looking suit and a diamond pin in his tie. Over there a woman with sleek furs around her shoulders.

His eyes settled on his mother sitting toward the back. Her coat was shabby and her hair was dull and straight. She sat with her shoulders hunched a little. But what a proud glow in her eye!

As soon as that graduation was over, do you know what he did? He rushed out the side door so he wouldn't have to be *embarrassed by his mother!*

Unthinkable! But, that's not a drop in the bucket compared to the kind of treatment a person gives God when we can look at the Father who loves us and see the price He paid because He loves us and turn our backs. If there's a spark of warmth in our hearts, any responsiveness at all, we look at Calvary and say, "Lord, I really want you to control my life. I want you to lift my burden of sin. I want you to give me hope. I want to be united with your Son, Jesus, in baptism. I want to be your child. I'm responding to your love."

---

[1] *Acts 17:22-32.*
[2] Boberg, Carl. "How Great Thou Art," Manna Music, Inc., 1955.

WHY DID JESUS HAVE TO DIE?

Twenty years ago this summer I was driving down a road in Southern Saskatchewan. A friend and myself were in a battered pick-up truck. That was the first time that I recall ever hearing this question asked. I had been preaching in a little country schoolhouse. The friend was not a Christian. He had been to every sermon. As we rolled along that afternoon he said, "You know, if what you are telling me is true, I need to do something about it. I'm just not real sure that it is true."

He got rather quiet for awhile, then he asked the question. "I don't understand why Jesus had to die. I don't understand why anyone had to die. Why did God do it that way? If someone had to die, why did it have to be Jesus?"

I frankly confess that I had no notion what the answer was. I wanted to very much. That was the first series of meetings I ever preached in, and the "friend" was my own brother-in-law.

I am still not sure I understand the deep implications of the question. But, I have considered the question long and carefully.

I would like to share some of the reasons why I think it is a good question and some of the answers I am finding.

Why *did* Jesus have to die? "For you know the grace of our Lord Jesus Christ, that though he was rich, yet for your sake he became poor, so that by his poverty you might become rich."[1] Why?

"Christ died for our sins in accordance with the scriptures."[2]

Why? Why *did* someone have to become poor? Why did *Jesus* have to die for us? It is a legitimate question.

If we are asking out of rebellion toward God, we will find no answer.

If we do not want God, we can find ample reason not to have Him. But, asking to understand God better will bring answers. "Seek," Jesus said, "and you will find."

At least part of the answer is tied up in the definition of three words. At first they appear to be sterile, religious, "preacher" words. But, let us attempt to see color and life in these words, as God intended.

The three words: Atonement, Reconciliation and Example.

ATONEMENT

Atonement! That's why Jesus had to die. That is why it had to be *Him.*

What does it mean? Actually, the word atonement says that someone paid a price for me that I am totally unable to pay for myself. Starkly, it means Jesus died for me because of my sin. I deserved death; Jesus died instead.

"But," you say, "Why did God make us sin to begin with, if He had to make such a stiff penalty for it." The answer to that one is easy. God did *not* make us sin. The Bible says,

> "Let no one say when he is tempted, 'I am tempted by God'; for God cannot be tempted with evil and he himself tempts no one; but each person is tempted when he is *lured and enticed by his own desire.* Then desire when it has conceived gives birth to sin; and sin when it is full-grown brings forth death."[2]

God did not make us sin. *We* surrendered to Satan's appeal to our self-deserving appetites.

"All right, I can see that, but why did God make it

possible for us to sin then. Why design us with the capacity for sin?" That is a large question. At least some of the answer is that God and men are alike. "God created man in His own image." One of those ways we are like God is that neither God nor man is complete without love. It is a miserable world if you have no one to love and no one to love you. God needs love and loved ones too. So He made man. See how important we are to him!

We can imagine that some of the things that went through the mind of God are similar to those that go through the mind of a parent. I have four children. I know that any one of them has the capacity to break my heart. I don't think they will break my heart, but they have that capacity. We knew that risk before we brought them into the world. But Carolyn and I wanted children badly enough we were willing to take the risk of their rebellion. We want them to love us, but we cannot force them to. Imagine if we brought our baby home from the hospital, lifted up her nightshirt and there on her back was a little dial. You set the needle on the words, "Love me," punch the button and she is programmed; Nothing she herself can do about it. Would this be a fulfilling relationship? We do not want her to love us because she *has* to; we want her to love us because she is free to.

When God made us He did not pre-program us either. We are not puppets on a string. He wants our love. He needs love so deeply He was willing to risk our creation, knowing our potential for rebellion. But He does not force us to love Him. He wants our relationship with him to be free and genuine. So he gave us the option: "to love" or "not to love." To choose "not to love" Him is at the root of what *sin* is all about. When we make that choice, we break God's heart.

So, Adam made the first choice. Sin is a tiny trickle that came out from under the gate of the Garden of Eden. That trickle grew into a stream, and that stream became a river. The river has become finally a mighty ocean, engulfing the whole human race. Paul says, "All have sinned and fall short of the glory of God."[3]

"None is righteous, no, not one."[4] There are consequences. "The wages of sin is death."[5]

"Yes, but why did He make the wages of sin so drastic? The death of Jesus or destruction for us? Why?"

The infinite mind will likely never grasp the total of the "why." But, some of the answer is obvious.

We are incapable of understanding how bad sin is. But God gives some indication of the destructive influence of sin since the penalty has to be so heavy.

When I was about four years old we did not have a refrigerator. The farm where I grew up still does not have a power line running to it. Then, the whole community had no electricity. So people kept the milk and the meat cool in the summertime in their ice houses. An ice house was a small cave in the side of the hill. It had a timber roof over it with a pile of straw on top of that. In the winter we cut great blocks of ice out of the ponds, put them in the ice house and buried them with straw and sawdust. With those two layers of insulation, the ice held through the summer.

So the ice house was vital to our way of life. No ice house—no meat and milk in the summer.

It was in the spring. Last year's grass was plenty dry. I was playing with some matches in that nice dry grass. The flame got so big that bare feet couldn't stomp it out. With the help of spring breezes the ice house was soon reduced to ashes!

Mother spanked me as hard as she could, but her spankings never were very persuasive. So she sent me to the field where my father was.

"You go tell him what you have done."

I ran to the field and rode the tractor with him.

He said, "Looks like something's burning down there."

I said, "Yeah, looks like something's burning down there."

But I never did get around to telling him about the ice house.

That night the door of my room opened and I sensed that "something was rotten in the state of Denmark." Dad sat on the edge of the bed and talked to me. He talked about ice houses and milk and meat and hot summers and maggots. I really did not get the significance of his message till he reached over and pulled down the covers. Then he pulled down the back of my flannel pajamas and with his calloused farmer hand, whaled the daylights out of me. I learned a lot more about the values of icehouses and milk and meat from that hard old hand than I did from the lecture he gave me.

Could this be why God has made the penalty of sin deep black? It is as if God said, "Here's how bad it is. I can't explain to you how bad it is. I said that 'the iniquities of the fathers are visited onto the children, unto the third and the fourth generation of them that hate me.' But, you still don't understand. You have seen the way it has wrecked the harmony of the world, the way it is breaking people's lives. You see the sorrow in homes and you see the emptiness in the eyes and you see the hopelessness at the grave. Even the universe is off balance. But you don't understand that. So, listen children. Sin is so bad, if you live in it, you will be separated from me forever."

"No," you say. "It just couldn't be. An eternity of punishment for only a lifetime of sin? It doesn't seem fair."

With a pistol it is possible to kill six people in six seconds. Would a just penalty be six seconds in the penitentiary? Would multiplying the penalty by ten be adequate—sixty seconds in prison? That is ten times as long as it took me to do the crime! Obviously ridiculous, isn't it! The worth of a deed cannot be measured by the length of time it takes to commit it. Nor can the impact of life in rebellion to God be measured by the length of time it takes to live it! The implications will affect generations yet unborn.

"It is incompatible with the love of God," you protest. "How could a loving God mete out that kind of penalty to creatures that He loves?"

How do you know that God loves you? You know it because the Bible says so. "God so loved the world."[6] If I can believe the Bible when it tells me that God loves me, then I can also believe the Bible when it says, "And they will go away into eternal punishment, but the righteous into eternal life."[7] The same Bible tells me of both the *wrath* and the *love* of God.

On the cross God is saying, with the life of His Son, "Sin is terrible." But at the same time He is saying, with the life of His Son, "I love you, and I'm paying the price for your sins."

You see, we don't have to dread the penalty of sin because no person here has to pay it, unless he chooses to. No one has to be lost. God wants us to be saved! That is why the Bible says, "Christ died for our sins."[8] Brother, that's good news!

I am a Canadian. But, I enjoy studying American history. I don't know that American history is more interesting than Canadian history, but you have a more interesting way of writing it down. However, there is one page of American history so black, it's shadow will be cast on generations yet to come. I refer to the time when one race of men was enslaved by another race of men.

At a slave auction on the lower Mississippi a group of slaves was led to the block. All of the humanity was worked and beaten out of them—they were like dreary dogs whose day is done.

But one young fellow stood tall and straight. His eyes had the light of deep intelligence. He had straight white teeth and the muscles rippled across his back. Of course, everyone wanted to buy him.

The bids kept rising. Finally an old farmer stepped out of the crowd. He had no shirt and no shoes. He bid a price so ridiculously high that the auctioneer let the gavel drop and said, "Sold."

The old farmer reached inside his bib overalls, produced a wad of bills and paid off the auctioneer. Then he laid his hand on the young slave's arm. The young man cursed at him and spit at him, "Why are you doing this to me?"

The old farmer said, "You don't understand. You see, that money I gave to the auctioneer was my entire life savings. I bought you so that I could set you free."

Don't you see this is what God has done? Christ was treated as we deserve, that we might be treated as He deserves. He died for our sins in which He had no part so that we could be justified by His righteousness in which we have no part. He received death that belonged to me, that I may gain the life that belongs to Him.

Isaiah was not exaggerating when he said,

"Surely he has borne our griefs and carried our sorrows; . . . he was -wounded for our transgressions, he was bruised for our iniquities; upon him was the chastisement that made us whole; . . . All we like sheep have gone astray; we have turned every one to his own way; and the Lord has laid on him the iniquity of us all."[9]

Do you know what this means to you? If you are to have any joy in your life now, any sense of forgiveness, any sense of destiny and purpose, *you have life* because *Jesus gave His* for you. That is what atonement means.

Why did it have to be Him? No one is good enough to be able to pay the price for his own sins, let alone all other people's sins as well. Animal sacrifice is not of significant enough value. "For it is impossible that the blood of bulls and goats should take away sins."[10] God selected the offering worth enough to pay, in that one event, the penalty of all the sins of all men of all history. The only one that was worth that much was Jesus. He is God's son. He was sinless. He could pay our debt.

> "He paid a debt He did not owe,
> I owed a debt I could not pay,
> I needed someone to wash my sins away.
> And now I sing a brand, new song—'Amazing Grace.'
> Christ Jesus paid a debt that I could never pay."
> (Anonymous)

RECONCILIATION

Now we come to that second word. The word is "reconcile" or "reconciliation." That is a second reason Jesus died. What does this word mean?

The word reconcile simply means "to bring together again things that have become separated." The price was paid for us, but it had to be paid in such a way that we would want to accept it. God was calling us back to Him by the event of the cross. We were alienated from God, not by His doing, but by our doing.

If I were to steal your car, I would make you my enemy. You might not know I had stolen it and still be nice to me. But my heart would say, "No, he's my enemy. I stole his car. You don't steal a car from your friend. He has to be my enemy." That is human nature.

It was not God who initiated sin and rebellion. He didn't cause the chasm between Himself and us. It was man.

> "Behold, the Lord's hand is not shortened, that it cannot save, or his ear dull, that it cannot hear; but your iniquities have made a separation between you and your God, and your sins have hid his face from you so that he does not hear."[11]

Man initiated this break between himself and God. We hunger for God, but have deluded ourselves into seeing God as our enemy. For this reason many sinful people seem almost angry at God. They see Him as a cosmic enemy. "The hound of Heaven is trying to run me down and make me pay for my sins."

Sometimes, at the death of a loved one, we say, "What did I do to deserve this?" That is not why our hearts are broken. God does not deal in that kind of personal vendetta. He wants us to come back to Him. But how could he effect that? He could not just crack a great lightning bolt at us and say, "You better get with me or else!" We would only be more deeply convinced that He is our enemy! So He devised the one beautiful way to do it. May I describe it best with another story?

George came home from work one day a little edgy. Mary said something he didn't like. He got angry and said some things he shouldn't. He hauled off and slapped her. He knocked her down, absolutely having taken leave of his senses. Then he stormed out the front door.

"Why in the world did I do that? I love that woman. I don't want to hurt that woman. But I did it."

Then he began building a wall in his mind.

"Yeah, I did it. She will *never* have anything to do with me anymore. You don't slap a woman around and have her still love you."

He pictured how bad she would hate him. He marched on down the street, around the corner into the bar and ordered a bottle to reinforce his idea that Mary was mad at him. He was becoming furious, not at himself, but at her for her hatred toward him. Imagine!

But something else was happening in Mary. She said, "No, that is not my husband. I don't want this to disrupt our home."

So she ran down the street shouting, "George, come back!"

He thought she was screaming threats at him. She tried all day to find him. She called. He wouldn't answer the phone.

"I know what she wants. She just wants to find out where I am so she can send the sheriff down here so they can put me in the jailhouse and bury the key. Do you know what I did to that woman?"

Finally, night time came. Throughout this sequence his beautiful, little four-year-old daughter had watched with those lovely, clear, innocent eyes.

Now her Mother said, "Susie, I want you to do something for me. I want you to go down to that part of town where I don't even like you to go in the daytime. Find Daddy and tell him that we love him and that we want him to come back home again."

Down through the dark Susie went. She was afraid. But she found her daddy.

He said, "What are you doing in here? Did your mother send you to spite me?" And she began to cry and threw her little arms around his neck.

"No, Daddy. Mother sent me here to tell you that we love you and we want you to come home again."

So he took that little hand down the street and up the front steps. There they met in the warm embrace of *reconciliation!* That is what reconciliation means.

Don't you see that in the cross of Jesus, this is what God was doing?

God looked out over the broken, rebellious world. How will I tell them I love them? How? Their ears are so full of rebellion and guilt that they cannot hear me. They have built walls. So He said, "Jesus, I have something I want you to do for me. I want you to go down into that world where you could even lose your soul." (You cannot tempt someone to do what he *cannot* do. The Bible says Jesus was "tempted in all points like we are.") He was sent down here by God to go through the dark streets and find us, and let us know the Father still loves us. Do you see why it had to be Him? Don't you see?

> "He is the head of the body, the church; he is the beginning, the first-born from the dead, that in everything he might be pre-eminent. For in him all the fullness of God was pleased to dwell, and through him to *reconcile* to himself all things, whether on earth or in heaven, making peace by the blood of his cross."[1][2]

It had to be Him.

Imagine being in Jerusalem the day the crucifixion took place. Someone is knocking on the door.

"Hey, come with me out to Golgotha. There's a crucifixion going on there."

"Bah, if you've seen one crucifixion, you've seen them all."

"No, no. This one is different. This man says that he is dying for God."

"Well, who is God mad at this time?"

"No, no. You don't understand. This one says that *he is God.*"

So I go down out of the gate and up to the hill. When I arrive at the cross, the sky has turned black, the earth begins to tremble, the rocks begin to crack open and lightning begins to lash the hill. Jesus says, "Father, forgive them because they don't know what they are doing." "Into your hands, I commit my spirit."

A hard-hearted old Roman soldier stands pallid and shaken and says, "This was the Son of god."

Things now begin to sink in. God isn't angry at me!!! He loves *me!!!* He *died* to let me know that he loves me.

Would you not want to fall at the foot of that cross and say, "Lord, here I am. Speak! Your servant is listening. Your wish is my command."

One could rise from the foot of the cross saying, "I'm saved by the grace of the *loving* God."

It had to be Him. The death of another man would only incite more resentment toward God. The death of an angel would go unnoticed in our world. But when God's son broke into my world and died on a cross, that means something! "The goodness of God leads me to repent."

EXAMPLE

Monday morning comes. So I'm a Christian. Where do I go from here? God loves me. God paid the price for my sins. So what? This brings us to that third word.

This third word is "example." Such a simple word. "For to this you have been called, because Christ also suffered for you, leaving you an example, that you should follow in his steps."[1][3]

Not only did Jesus die to pay for our sins and do that in a way that would reconcile us to God, but he calls us to follow His example. The cross a symbol of *forgiveness.* It is also a symbol of a *life style.* He is saying, "Follow me into suffering, follow me into death. Die to live."

How was God to get us to do His will, to be like he wanted us to be? First, he left us on our own to seek him. Finally, Jeremiah said, "Lord, I know that the ways of a man are not within himself. It is not within man that walks to direct his own steps."

We blew the whole thing.

So God said, "All right, I'll give you a law. Thou shalt do this, and thou shalt not do that . . . " There is no life in a law. We broke the law. All it did was show us our weaknesses.

So finally God said, "All right, now I'll show you what I mean." We could not understand the voice of God or the mind of God. If He wrote across the sky in a divine language, how could the human mind comprehend that?

Preachers used to put the children on the front seats before the services started to learn Bible songs. One of the old classics is "The Wise Man Built His House Upon the Rock."

Now imagine: "All right, kids, we are going to learn about the wise man who built his house on the rock. When I say 'the wise man,' you extend the index finger of your right hand toward your right temple at a *45°* angle from your head, two inches in front of your ear. When I say 'built his house on the rock,' you extend your left hand, palm up, with the clenched fist of your right hand resting on the upturned palm of your left hand . . . "

Do you suppose the kids would follow me? Let's suppose there was one sharp little fellow who understood. Do you think he would try to do it? He would be afraid he had misunderstood. He is not going to make a fool of himself.

So what do I do? I just say, "The wise man built his house upon the rock and the rains came tumbling down." And as I *say* it, I *act it out myself.* Then they do it. Why? Because they understand exactly what I mean and they have the courage to try it because I did it first!

That is what Jesus came into the world to do. We are like little children. He *showed* us how to live, as well as telling us. The whole life of Jesus is teaching me to sing a beautiful song, and He is giving me the courage to try it because He did it first.

> Jesus came singing love,
> He lived singing love,
> He died singing love,
> He rose in silence.

If the song is continued, we must do the singing!

Contemplate the impact of His life!

In the city of Philippi, Paul and Silas learned of some ladies praying down by the river. They went and taught them about Jesus and baptized them. Then they went regularly to their prayer meetings.[14]

A girl with an evil spirit would follow along behind them saying, "These men are servants of the most High God." She was a fortune teller who brought her masters a good deal of money. Paul cast the evil spirit out of her. Her owners became angry. They had lost their source of income. They stirred folks against Paul and Silas. Paul and Silas were brought into the town square and beaten.

We are not sure whether the beating was with rods, (lictors), or with the whip, (flagellum). But because "they commanded" them beaten, it is implied that they were handed over to the provincial officer, the Roman jailor.

Roman jailors were not hired because they knew how to keep keys away from jailbirds. They were men who, from their very childhood, were schooled in the art of cruelty. They had beautiful whips braided with gold, studded with jewels. The lash was several feet long. At the tip would be one tongue with a piece of metal in it and another with a piece of bone and another with a thorn, etc.

The victim would be stripped and his wrists bound to his ankles so his back was fully exposed. The "jailor" would step off the right distance. When he laid on the whip, it would pop with such precision when skillfully handled, as to tear chunks of flesh from a man's back. Sometimes the victim's ribs would be peeled by the scourging.

The Bible says Paul and Silas were put in the prison with their feet in the stocks.

At midnight they sat bleeding in a dungeon infested by rats, lice, and stench, with their feet in stocks. Do you know what they were doing? Were they saying, "Well, I guess I stuck my neck out too far this time? I should have gone a little slower with the people."

Is that what they said? Never! The Bible says they were *singing hymns.* The jailor was listening. Can you imagine what went through his mind?

"I tore the hides off those men's backs. They don't know when they will get out of this place. And they are *singing?"*

The earthquake came. The prisoner's chains were broken. The whole prison was a shambles. I can hear people screaming and running about in confusion.

Of course, the jailor thought all was lost. He was responsible for the prison with his life. He took a sword and was going to commit suicide.

Through that darkness and pandemonium the voice of Paul was heard, "Don't you hurt yourself. Everyone is still here." I can see the jailor freeze in his tracks.

"How did he know that? It is dark in here. He does not even know how many prisoners there are. But I believe him."

He called for lights and said, "What must I to do to be saved."

Paul said, "If you believe in the Lord Jesus Christ, you will be saved."

What did he know about the Lord Jesus Christ? So Paul told him about Jesus. If ever there was a single sermon I would like to have heard, that would have been it. I do not know all he told him, but he told him about the Lord Jesus. When he finished, "The jailor took them the same hour of the night, *washed their stripes* and was baptized."[1][5]

Did you notice the first part? Washed their stripes! The hand that had wielded the lash of cruelty now was carrying a sponge of mercy. What power in the Lord Jesus Christ and his example. I cannot imagine that jailor ever taking up the lash again.

This is the impact of Jesus. No one else could be like that. No one else could love like Him and die like Him. It had to be Him. Jesus. *He* paid for my sins. *He* called me back to a God that loves me. *He* showed me how to live my life the best way. That is where my hope originates. If I will just take hold of his hand, turn away from myself and be buried with him in baptism, he will give me a new life. I can follow Him.

"It was battered and scarred and the auctioneer thought it
     scarcely worth his while,
To wast his time on the old violin. So, he held it up with a
     smile,
'How much am I bidden, good folks,' he cried,
'Who'll start the bidding for me?'
'A dollar. A dollar, who'll make it two.'
'Two dollars.' 'Who'll make it three?'
"Three dollars once, three dollars twice, going for three.'
     But no,
From the room far back a gray-haired man came forward,
     picked up the bow
Wiping the dust from the old violin, and tightening all the
     strings,
He played a melody, sweet and low
As rich as an angel sings.
The music throbbed and each heart nigh burst
And the old man's face was aglow
Every soul was warmed clean through
By the melody sweet and low.

The music stopped. The auctioneer
In a voice that was quiet and low
Said, 'How much now for the old violin?'

And he picked it up with the bow.
'A thousand.' 'A thousand. Who'll make it two?'
'Two thousand.' 'Who'll make it three?'
'Three thousand once, three thousand twice,
Going and gone,' said he.
The people cheered. But, some of them said, 'We don't
    quite understand
What changed it's worth.' Came the swift reply,
'It was the touch of the master's hand.'

And there is many a man with his life out of tune
All battered and scarred with sin,
Who is auctioned cheap to a thoughtless crowd,
Just like the old violin.
Mess of pottage, glass of wine,
A game and he travels on,
He's going once, going twice,
Going and almost gone,
But the Master comes, and the foolish crowd,
Never can quite understand
The worth of a soul, or the change that's wrought
By the touch of the Master's hand."

Why not let him touch your life? Give yourself to Him
right now

---

[1] *II Corinthians 8:9.*
[2] *I Corinthians 15:3*
[2] *James 1:13-15.*
[3] *Romans 3:23.*
[4] *Romans 3:10.*
[5] *Romans 6:23.*
[6] *John 3:16.*
[7] *Matthew 25:46.*
[8] *I Corinthians 15:3.*
[9] *Isaiah 53:4-6.*
[10] *Hebrews 10:4.*
[11] *Isaiah 59:1-2.*
[12] *Colossians 1:18-20.*
[13] *I Peter 2:21.*
[14] *Acts 16:11-34.*
[15] *Acts 16:33.*

MISUNDERSTANDINGS ABOUT THE CHURCH

"These words of Peter moved them deeply, and they said to him and to the other apostles, 'Brothers, what should we do?' And Peter replied, 'Each one of you must turn from sin, return to God, and be baptized in the name of Jesus Christ for the forgiveness of your sins; then you also shall receive this gift, the Holy Spirit. For Christ promised Him to each one of you who has been called by the Lord our God, and to your children and even to those in distant lands!' Then Peter preached a long sermon, telling about Jesus and strongly urging all his listeners to save themselves from the evils of their nation. And those who believed Peter were baptized—about 3,000 in all! They joined with the other believers in regular attendance at the apostles' teaching sessions and at the Communion services and prayer meetings. A deep sense of awe was on them all, and the apostles did many miracles. And all the believers met together constantly and shared everything with each other, selling their possessions and dividing with those in need. They worshiped together regularly at the Temple each day, met in small groups in homes for Communion and shared their meals with great joy and thankfulness, praising God. The whole city was favorable to them, and each day God added to them all who were being saved."[1]

This lesson is designed for all people who love the Lord, whether they are members of the church of Christ or not. I am convinced, you are honest people. Folks don't go to church and try to find out about Jesus unless they have an honest desire to be what God wants them to be. Consequently, we will deal with some rather delicate issues in a forthright manner. I believe you are going to struggle at least as hard to understand what I am trying to say as I am going to struggle to say it clearly.

Communication *is* delicate and I might not always say what I want to say. One preacher had this difficulty. A couple wanted to get married after the Sunday evening services. The preacher was to invite everyone to stay. Sunday evening came. The service was ended with the "Amen." After that the preacher said, "Now will those who wanted to get married please come forward." The young couple came forward and seven old maids came with them! What one *means* to say and what another *perceives* them to say are often quite different. It is our aim now to discuss *misunderstandings* concerning the church of Christ.

Even this expression is open for misunderstanding. It could seem to imply folks here are so dull that they can't understand what the church is. We certainly don't mean to imply that.

To others it may sound like we're saying, "You are so prejudiced you don't want to understand." We don't mean that either.

It could well be that most of the misunderstandings about the churches of Christ are our own doing.

For example, there are people who profess to be part of our fellowship who don't have a clear concept of what we are trying to do. They just accidentally stumbled into this fellowship. Others simply went to the church nearest to them, and call themselves members of it. They don't understand what we are really trying to be. You could easily have gotten misimpressions from such people. That wouldn't be your fault.

Then there are people who are associated with us, and they understand very well what we are trying to do, but through an improper attitude or an unfortunate choice of words, may express only a bigoted, twisted caricature of what our plea is. If you misunderstand because of such a person, this wouldn't be your fault either!

We realize misunderstandings will arise and we accept blame for them. That is why we attempt here to clear away some misunderstandings.

THE CHURCH IN THE BIBLE IS SACRED

There is another reason I am proud to attempt clarification. Churches are not just religious clubs. Christians didn't individually indentify with Jesus, a long time ago, and then decide, "Well, wouldn't it be nice to have a Christian's club," which later evolved into an institution called a church. That's not what the church is.

The church is prominent in the Bible. It was a simple fellowship of believers, yet it was a dream in the mind of God before He even created this world. He took long centuries to bring about the proper conditions for the church to be born.

Jesus himself said, "I will build my church."[2] Later the scriptures say Jesus was "adding the people to the church."[3] The Bible tells us Jesus loved his church like a husband and wife love each other.[4] And to some elders he said, "Take heed to yourselves and to all the flock . . . to care for the church of God which he obtained with the blood of his own Son."[5] That is how special the church is to the heavenly Father and to His Son, Jesus Christ.

So, you see, to me it's a real honor to speak on behalf of the church.

"THE ONLY ONES SAVED?"

One of the misunderstandings people occasionally reflect is this: "You can talk of this one church in the Bible. Is it true then that you think that you are the only ones that are going to go to heaven and everybody else is going to go to hell?"

I don't remember ever having heard any of our preachers get up and say that. If it happened I don't believe that such an attitude is becoming to Christians, for several reasons.

In the first place, not all of "our bunch" are going to make it. The Bible says,

"The Son of man will send his angels, and they will gather out of his kingdom," (that's out of the church, out of the body of people that Jesus saved), "all causes of sin and all evildoers, and throw them into the furnace of fire; there men will weep and gnash their teeth."[6]

This passage very plainly says there are some "church members" who are not what God wants them to be. Some quit trusting and obeying and turn back to living for themselves. So a baptismal certificate from a church of Christ is not a valid sign that one is a child of God or in good standing.

Secondly, God didn't give human beings the responsibility to judge the destiny of other people. We don't have that kind of wisdom. We don't have that kind of justice. We don't have that kind of mercy.

Probably, if I were to do the judging, those I like would be all right, but the ones that strike me the wrong way might be in trouble.

God, however, is not partial. God is so merciful that He sent his own Son to die for me. I can let my weight down confidently on the mercy of a God that would do that. If we are in the business of making ecclesiastical pronouncements about people's eternal destinies, we ought to repent before God for assuming a prerogative that belongs to Him alone.

Let me be clear, however. This doesn't mean we don't have any idea about whether or not we are saved. God didn't leave this up for grabs. He told us exactly what the basis of His judgment would be.

Jesus said, "He who rejects me and does not receive my sayings has a judge; the word that I have spoken will be his judge on the last day."[7] The Bible reveals God's criterion for judgment. He will judge us on the basis of what He says in the scriptures.

YOU MEAN, EXACTLY CORRECT?

Someone says, "Does that mean then that if I really tried to follow the Bible, and I honestly wanted to serve God, but I misunderstood an important concept here or there that God would destroy me?"

Of course, that's up to God. The answer to this is beyond my depth. But are we forced to assume that God has that kind of a harsh, legalistic approach to things? My whole salvation is based on the trust that God's *mercy is broader than God's law*. Why? Because I am not intelligent enough to understand all of it or good enough to obey all of it. The only hope I have is His mercy, His grace.

> "For by grace you have been saved through faith; and this is not your own doing, it is the gift of God—not because of works, lest any man should boast."*Eph. 2:8-9*(RSV)

However, that could be presumed upon. Imagine that you run a traffic light.

The officer tickets you.

The judge says, "Did you see the red light?"

"Yes, sir."

"Well, do you know what a red light means?"

"Yes, sir, I do, but you see I had my wife in the car. She was having a heart attack and the doctor has said, 'If that happens, get her to oxygen quick as you can.' I wasn't concerned about little things like red lights, Your Honor."

Now, if the judge believes you, he may, *because of extenuating circumstances,* (and, because of his mercy), let you off. He might not exact the fine. But, if he doesn't, the law will still read the same way. And you won't be granted the right to ignore all traffic lights from here on in.

Because God is a merciful God doesn't give me the right

to say, "Well, it doesn't matter. I won't worry about trying to know and do His will. He's merciful anyway. I'll just plead his mercy, and run roughshod over what he has said." God wants us to do what is right, what is in harmony with what the Bible says.

THE ONLY ONES WHO ARE RIGHT?

"Well," one man said, "Maybe I should rephrase that. You *do* believe, though, that you are the only ones who are right, and everyone else is wrong. Is that the case?"

Anyone who teaches that Jesus Christ is God's son is right about that. Anyone who teaches the Bible is God's complete revelation to man is preaching what's true . . . about that. He may not be right on everything, but he's right on that. It would be so pompous then to say, "Well, I guess maybe I am the only fellow that's right."

Myself, our fellowship, my brothers don't claim to have any monopoly on brains. Nor do we claim a corner on sincerity. There are many, many other wonderfully intelligent and fine people throughout the world that certainly put me to shame in studying the word of God.

I frankly confess to you. I know that there are times I've stood in the pulpit and preached things that weren't true. As I discover where I'm wrong, it is my aim to keep on correcting things. But, I don't always know at the time when I've said something that isn't true. I have such limited understanding. I have no doubt, as life goes on, I'll keep on teaching things that aren't true until someone helps make them straight. But that is beside the issue.

The point, of course, comes down to, "What does the Bible say?" Truth is desperately important.

When the astronauts returned from the moon on their last journey, it really mattered about *how they re-entered* the earth's atmosphere. If they came in more than two degrees too shallow an angle, they could bounce off the atmosphere into the blackness of space and never be heard from again. If they came in more than two degrees too sharp an angle, speed would create such friction heat that they would be burned to a crisp. So they had to be right, within a four-degree differential. Truth was vital to survival!

The same God that made the physical laws of the universe made our spiritual universe and ourselves as well. He understands how we tick. In the Bible he says, "Do it this way."

If we get too far from God, things don't go right. Truth is desperately important. I don't know how many "degrees of differential" God allows before He rejects us. Our salvation is dependent on his mercy and grace, not on our absolute correctness. But that doesn't mean truth isn't desperately, urgently important. God's grace is not extended to those who reject His truth and rebel against it.

Some years ago I was in Tennessee in gospel meetings. A man coming to the meetings was a preacher for one of the denominations in the community. Wonderful man. He was a big man with a great deep voice and a heart that filled his huge chest. He always called me "little preacher." (I never did argue with him about that!)

I went over to his house to visit with him one afternoon. He was very warm and complimentary.

"Well now, little preacher," he said, "I like the things you have been saying. But there is just one thing that bothers me. You seem to think you are the only one who's right, and everyone else is wrong."

I was embarrassed down to the toes of my shoes. He had read me correctly.

I apologized, "Sir, I don't really want to leave that impression. But, help me, sir. Do you believe the Bible is one unified truth? Or do you believe that God said one thing to one person and something contradictory to another person on the same subject, but both statements are true? Or do you believe the Bible is one unified message?"

He said, "The Bible is one unified message. God doesn't speak with 'forked tongue.'"

I asked, "You preach every Sunday, don't you?"

He said, "Yes, I do."

I said, "When you preach do you believe that you are preaching that one unified truth that's in the Bible?"

He said, "Yes sir. I'd be a hypocrite to preach something I really didn't think was God's truth."

By now I had really come to feel at home with the fellow. I said, "Shake my hand, because I feel just like you do about that. I believe there is one unified truth in the Bible. And, before God, I believe that's what I'm preaching."

"It really doesn't matter what I preach or what you preach. The issue is, 'What does the Bible say?' What does God say about it? That's the solid place."

If we'll read the New Testament, reflect on it and pray about it and let God's Spirit speak to us through the New Testament, we'll be what God wants us to be.

ONLY THE NEW TESTAMENT

"But, " someone says, "Just a minute now. You raise another question. New Testament! You have mentioned that repeatedly. *New Testament Christianity.* It must be right, then, that you don't believe in the Old Testament. Correct?"

Because we *do* frequently use the expression "New Testament Christianity," a misimpression could occur. But, the reason we express things that way is not because we don't believe in the Old Testament. The Old Testament *is* God's word. It would be impossible to really understand the New Testament without it. A good deal of the terminology in the New Testament is developed from the Old Testament.

There are great examples and lessons in the Old Testament by which men of faith live today. But, when we read the Old Testament it's like reading a letter to someone else. It was primarily written to the Jewish people. It was in *preparation* for the time when Jesus was to come. But the church, you see, *is* the church of the *Lord Jesus*. Christians are followers of the *Lord Jesus*. And the *Lord Jesus* wasn't even born until 450 years after the Old Testament had been completed. The Jews have never been followers of Jesus. The New Testament picks up on the historical development and the prophetic statements of the Old Testament and explains many of them. The intent of many New Testament references to Old Testament passages is, "This is what I was referring to. Now it has come. Here's my plan for you, my power for you—in the New Testament."

The Bible says that Jews and Gentiles were once divided.,

> "But now in Christ Jesus you who once were far off have been brought near in the blood of Christ, for he is our peace, who has made us both one, and has broken down the dividing wall of hostility, by abolishing in his flesh the law of commandments and ordinances, that he might create in himself one new man in place of the two, so making peace."[8]

The ritual that belonged to the Hebrews, and the law that belonged to the Jews were fulfilled when Jesus died. He gave us direct relationship to Him through His blood of the New Testament. Jew and Gentile are now one in Him, in His church. That's why we talk about *New Testament* Christians.

If we'll do what the New Testament says, do it with the mind, do it with the body, do it with the heart, do it with the will, do it from the very depth of our hearts, we'll be God's people.

SAVED BY WORKS?

"That raises another question," someone says. "You have really come down hard on this word 'do.' I guess, then, you believe that we are saved by doing good works."

No! If we were to tell you that you could be saved by doing good works, we would be flatly contradicting what the Bible says! We can't lift ourselves to heaven by out bootstraps. If we did *good* from the time we are one year old to the time we are one hundred and one years old, twenty-five hours a day, we couldn't earn five minutes in heaven!

"He saved us, not because of deeds done by us in righteousness, but in virtue of his own mercy, by the washing of regeneration and renewal in the Holy Spirit."[9]

"For by grace you have been saved through faith; and this is not your own doing, it is the gift of God—not because of works, lest any man should boast."[10]

When he has made us a "new creation," we are created in Christ *for good works*. But the good works are the *result* of salvation, not the *means to it*.

We can't do enough good to *offset* the bad that's in us because of our sin. All of us are sinners. The world is full of sinners. The church is full of sinners. But, there are two kinds of sinners in the world—*lost sinners* and *saved sinners*.

What's the difference between a lost sinner and a saved sinner?

The difference isn't necessarily that the lost sinner is a "bad guy" and the saved sinner is a "real good fellow." It is true that when the claims of Christ are made on us and the Holy Spirit begins to live in us, we begin to become transformed into the image of Jesus. But for some of us this is a pitifully slow job. I live in that struggle every day. On the other hand, there are some wonderful, good people—good citizens, people whose company one would enjoy—who don't know Jesus Christ. One cannot always tell the lost from the saved people by how much good they do. In the church there are going to be emotionally weak people. So I must not assume that every time a church member is doing bad things that I should scream, "Hypocrite!" I know my own weaknesses. Yet, I know I want to serve God. My will has been committed to God. I am also weak and blind. Many of us, struggling along, are saved by the mercy and grace of God, but are terribly weak.

But what's the difference then? The difference is that when the judgement day comes the *saved sinners* will stand before God with all of their sins covered and hidden by the grace of God through Jesus Christ! The *lost sinners* will simply have to stand there with their bare sins hanging out. That's the difference.

You ask, "How do you have your sins covered by the grace of God?" This is where the key comes in. The power that saves us is God's grace. But we have to *accept* that grace. We have to *receive* the power.

Somewhere there is a dynamo that is producing electricity which is making these lights glow. There is no power in the light bulb, and there is no power in the switch. However, if you don't have the switch on, the lights won't glow! Yet one could fasten a bushel basket of light switches to one light bulb, and it wouldn't accomplish anything. The power is not in the switch. There is no power in a switch, but the switch must be on before the light receives power from the dynamo.

The power to save is in the grace of God. The way we "flip the switch" is through obedient faith, trusting response.

The Bible says, "He that believes and is baptized shall be saved."[11] That is flipping the switch. It is not generating power. It is simply opening the way for God's power to come through. That's why Peter said, "Repent and be baptized

every one of you in the name of Jesus Christ *for the forgiveness* of your sins; and *you will receive the gift of the Holy
Spirit.*"[1][2] Trust and obey, and open the way for *God's*
power to do its saving.

SAVED BY WATER?

"That brings me to another question," someone may
respond. "You mentioned baptism twice. Is it true, then, that
you believe we are saved by water?"

Impossible! There *is* a detergent that can wash away the
stain of sin, but it's not water and it's not New, Blue Cheer,
or Mr. Clean either. There's only one detergent of which the
Bible speaks that can wash away our sin. "The blood of Jesus
Christ cleanses us from our sin."[1][3]

Problem: How many of us have ever seen the blood of
Jesus? When we visited Palestine last year, we never were sure
we had found the exact hill where Jesus was crucified.
Suppose we *had* found the hill and I could draw an "X" in
the dirt right where the cross stood. If we were to dig all over
that hill, we would never find any of the blood of Jesus.
Time has taken care of that.

But suppose we did find, not just a drop, not just a
bucketful, but a whole swimming pool full of the blood of
Jesus Christ. To take a running jump right into the middle of
it wouldn't give any assurance whatsoever of sins washed
away. God didn't promise that the literal, physical blood of
Jesus applied to the external of my literal, physical body
would do anything for the *spiritual contamination of my
soul.* The blood cleansing is a spiritual event; "figurative," if
you choose to use that word. But spiritually we need to
contact the shed blood of Jesus.

This next thought or two may sound ridiculous if you
are thinking literally and physically. We are speaking figuratively. If I am to get to the blood of Jesus, I'll need to get
into the situation where the blood was shed. Jesus' blood was

shed *in His death* on the cross. The Roman soldier opened Jesus' side with a spear and blood poured out. It was a death experience that poured out the blood of Jesus. So if I am to contact the blood of Jesus to have my soul washed, I must somehow enter the death of Jesus.

This really sounds strange, right? But, remember we're thinking figuratively now, spiritually. *How* am I to get into the death of Jesus to contact the blood, the cleansing agent? Rather than speculate on it, turn your Bible to *Romans chapter 6.* It's very clear.

> "How can we who died to sin still live in it? Do you not know that all of us who have been baptized into Christ Jesus were baptized into his death? We were *buried therefore with him by baptism into death,* so that as Christ was raised from the dead by the glory of the Father, we too might walk in newness of life."[14]

Further in the chapter Paul summarized this:

> "But thanks be to God, that you who *were* once slaves of sin have become obedient from the heart to the standard of teaching to which you were committed, and, having been set free from sin, *have become* slaves of righteousness."[15]

Isn't that clear? God's not trying to confuse anyone. He doesn't want anyone lost.

IS THE GOSPEL A "MECHANISM"?

"Clear it is," someone says, "But it almost seems mechanical. It seems cold. This confirms the rumor that you people don't really believe in heartfelt religion."

If we've come this far with that understanding we've missed the whole point. Water baptism is a physical and external expression of what is at that moment spiritually taking place in the heart.

When the people on Pentecost day heard about Jesus,

they said, "What will we do?" He said, "Your hearts need to be changed. You need to *repent* and you need to be *baptized* in the name of Jesus. Then you will receive forgiveness of your sins and the gift of the Holy Spirit." There is powerful change in men's hearts when they are cleansed by the blood of Jesus!

"Christianity" suffers terrible problems today because folks are looking for an external formula that will make Christians out of people. Jesus calls for us to totally abandon ourselves. He said,

> "And you shall love the Lord your God with all your heart, and with all your soul, and with all your mind, and with all your strength. The second is this, You shall love your neighbor as yourself. There is no other commandment greater than these."[16]

> "Because, if you confess with your lips that Jesus is Lord and believe in your heart that God raised him from the dead, you will be saved. For man believes with his heart and so is justified, and he confesses with his lips and so is saved.[17]

The fundamental change in conversion is a changed heart.

OUR PLEA

Don't you see, then, that our aim is simply and plainly to look in the Bible for the basic essence of Christianity. We want to respond to that, to teach that, to obey that. We must make the cultural transition from the first to the twentieth century, but still retain the essential, Biblical, basic, life-giving ingredients. That's what we want to do. We want to teach what they taught. We want to function like they functioned. We want to worship like they worshipped. We want to move together in the same system that they did. We want to preach the same terms of salvation. We want to be filled with the same Spirit and simply be God's people, that's all. We want to be Christians without bowing before any denomination whatsoever.

"That sounds real good to me," someone says, "But why then did you join the Church of Christ?"

The only religious organization I've ever joined in my life was a religious book club. I have never joined any denomination. I never made application and asked for some people to receive me on their terms. Jesus said, "If you believe and are baptized, you will be saved." I believe that. I responded to that so He saved me. Then, the scripture says, "The Lord added to their number day by day those who were being saved."[18] And I trust God for that. If I'm saved, I *am* part of *His* church. And what people think about it doesn't really matter. God promised that. So I've never really "joined up" with any institutional religion.

"How did you get to preaching for this group, then?"

You see, in spite of all of our hang-ups and problems and our blind spots, we're simply trying to be a free people in Jesus. Our fellowship wants to be folks who long since abandoned any allegiance to human religious systems, as far as they could understand how. Others have deliberately chosen to be Christians without joining any man-made religious group. That's what our aim, our purpose, our struggle is. We invite you to help us find the fullness of that. We want to keep uncovering and recovering the basic religion of Jesus Christ as revealed in the scriptures. We want to cultivate only that.

Look at it this way! You are sitting on a creek bank fishing. You hear a noise—a car coming up the gravel road. It is a brand new convertible. There are two people in it. One is driving. The other one has a Bible in his hand and he is talking to the driver. When they get to the creek, the driver shuts off the engine.

He says, "Well, here is water. What keeps me from being baptized?"

The fellow with the Bible says, "If you believe in Jesus, you can."

"Why, I believe that."

So they get out of the car, walk down into the water and the fellow who had the Bible baptizes the fellow who had the steering wheel. They come up out of the water and the driver gets back into his car and drives away singing "Amazing Grace." Beautiful experience. Beautiful, simple scene.

Two questions! What group would you say that fellow represented who did the preaching? What church would you say the fellow who was baptized became a member of?

Answer: "Well, I guess it would be one of your bunch."

That's right. All we've done is reach into *Acts chapter 8* to the story about Philip and the eunuch. We lifted it from that old chariot and put it into a new convertible. All of the other essential facts are just the same.

Only, I would rather turn it around. I would rather be part of *His* bunch. I want to be a part of the same church that eunuch became a member of that day. I want to be a part of the same body as Philip, who did the baptizing that day. We want to be a part of the church that Paul was a part of. We want to function as a body the way that body functioned in Corinth and Ephesus and Troas in New Testament times. We just want to be a part of that church. We want enough confidence in Jesus to declare what's true, even if it costs us our lives as it did Stephen.

Wouldn't it be beautiful, wouldn't it be great if we could just do that in this community? If we could forget all of our differences, throw out all of the sectarian stipulations and troubling traditions we've drawn up, and just be Christians. We could have a *few* great buildings in this happy community and people could worship *together*. All of the money we're spending on preachers who compete with each other could be saved and sent to preach the gospel to someone who has never heard it. There would be a force in America that would make Satan shiver in his boots. The Bible says, "They'll know that you are my children if you love each other." And "the earth would tremble beneath our tread and echo with our shout!" It's a beautiful dream.

Why not come with us tonight to help us realize the dream. Come with us to the Bible and come with our Bibles in a search for Jesus. Come tonight and respond to His will.

---

[1] Living New Testament, *Acts 2:37-47.*
[2] *Matthew 16:18.*
[3] *Acts 2:47.*
[4] *Ephesians 5:25ff.*
[5] *Acts 20:28.*
[6] *Matthew 13:41-42.*
[7] *John 12:48.*
[8] *Ephesians 2:13-15.*
[9] *Titus 3:5.*
[10] *Ephesians 2:8-9.*
[11] *Mark 16:16.*
[12] *Acts 2:38.*
[13] *I John 1:7.*
[14] *Romans 6:2-4.*
[15] *Romans 6:17-18.*
[16] *Mark 12:30-31.*
[17] *Romans 10:9-10.*
[18] *Acts 2:47.*

EXPERIENCING THE CHURCH

Some 350 years ago, settlers landing on the eastern seaboard of this nation established a townsite. They elected a town government. The town government decided that they would build a road five miles into the wilderness. The villagers wanted to impeach the new government because they said they didn't need a road like that. "Who wants to go five miles westward into the wilderness?"

It is amazing that a people could have lost their pioneering spirit so quickly. Folks had enough pioneering spirit to see *3,000 miles* across an ocean, but had lost it so quickly, that in two years they couldn't see *five miles* across a continent.

You know, something like this has happened to the Church. There was a day when it was small, but it was alive. It was a dynamic fellowship of people who upset the world with explosive and disturbing ideas. Some despised the Christians, some followed the Christians, but no one could ignore the Christians. It's different today.

An English churchman stated it very well, I think, "You know, I can't figure out what happened. When Paul went somewhere they had a riot. When I go they have a cup of tea." What *has* happened to the Church of Jesus?

In the letters to the Colossians, the Ephesians, the Romans, the Corinthians and in other New Testament passages we see the Church of the Lord described as His *body*. There is a large truth upon which we can draw here.

Jesus is not physically in the world anymore. He lives in our hearts spiritually. But, He *is here!* We are His body. We are actually the physical manifestation of Jesus in the world.

What did Jesus do when He was physically in the world?

He "went about doing good." His eyes and feet were always "seeking the lost." He "loved," had "compassion." "Jesus wept." He "thirsted," "was hungry." He was a *real* part of His world. He was not just in the synagogue, but in the market-place, the seaside, the mountains, the crowded streets and the dirty roadways as well. He was "God *with us.*"

If we *are* the living body of Jesus, what *will* we be doing? Is the "body" of Jesus today fulfilling His purposes in the world?

WHAT IS HIS "LIVING BODY" DOING

In the first place, *a living body feels.* I saw a living body once that didn't feel. In one of the congregations where I was holding a meeting, an elder carried on his own business, lived a normal life, except that he had one peculiar problem. He had no sense of feeling. He couldn't put the keys in his automobile in the dark because he couldn't feel for that spot like you can. He couldn't drive his automobile without hanging tightly to the wheel, because if he lost it, he couldn't catch it again, by feel, like *you* can.

One day he was getting out of his truck. As he started to walk away, he was pulled up with a jerk. He had slammed his thumb in the door and didn't know it. He turned around to open the door, and when he turned back there was a lady that had fainted dead away. She just couldn't handle that.

There is something wrong with a body that doesn't feel. A living body feels. How many times do the gospels say of Jesus, "He had compassion," or "He looked at them and loved them"?

I'm not talking about some sort of emotional feeling. Love is feeling strongly enough that we can act properly. It is the will to perform in another's best interest at no matter what cost to ourselves. I'm talking about compassion, that always serves.

See how *I Cor. 13:* begins: "Though I speak with the tongues of men and of angels and have not love, it doesn't profit me anything." We are a people who exalt good *oratory.* The great man of God is the great speaker. We have become "ecclesiastical gourmets," and "sermon samplers." To some, good "religion" is to experience good preaching.

Paul shows this to be irrelevant, without love. Paul further said, "If I have the gift of prophecy, and know all mystery and knowledge, but don't have love, it doesn't profit me."

We exalt *knowledge* too, don't we? If one is not a good speaker, to have any recognition in our fellowship, he surely must be a scholar! However, Paul said I can know a lot of things, but if I don't love, I'm nothing.

He even said I can be sacrificial. "I can give away everything I own," (that should be a test of real commitment, shouldn't it) "even give my body to be burned," but if it is not to serve the object of God's love, it is only the ultimate in self-glorification.

We must be a fellowship that *feels* if we are the living body of Jesus in the world.

The compelling force of the early church was their love. "By this," Jesus said, "all men will know that you are my disciples, because you love one another." When the folks had been bruised long enough by the law of the "survival of the fittest" in a dog-eat-dog world, a fellowship of love was irresistible like a green oasis in the dry desert of life. "Lo, how they loved one another, " was the observation of one amazed onlooker.

LIVING BODY GROWS

The living body not only feels, but the living body grows. Some months ago, I met a strange girl in a high school. She sat in a wheel chair and her feet didn't even hang over the edge. She was 18 years old. There was something wrong, wasn't there? Because a living body grows.

How many times does the New Testament say, "The number of the disciples grew"? Three thousand were baptized. Five thousand were *"added"* to the Lord. The number of disciples *"multiplied."* "So mightily grew the word of the Lord and prevailed."

There was something about the nature of that fellowship that kept expanding. Not necessarily talented speakers and efficient programs, but because each one of the people in that fellowship had something that he could not resist sharing. Each had "tasted that the Lord is gracious."

The Church in the Bible is never described as an *institution.* It isn't called an *organization.* It is fundamentally and basically an "organism," a fellowship. It is a community of people who are bound together by their love for Jesus, not ecclesiastically regimented or made all to conform by being run through the same theological screen. So they were not exclusive, but inclusive in mentality, organization and life style.

I saw a young girl reach out in a way I haven't seen anyone reach out in a long time. Her name was Anna Vininni. Anna was reared as a Roman Catholic, but she had never met Jesus. She got her life tangled in the drug scene, addicted to heroin. Sometime back, after several suicide attempts, she came to the realization that Jesus was real. She still didn't know what He wanted her to do. Later she was baptized into Christ, and immediately she went to all of her neighbors and friends. Within two weeks she had led five people to Jesus Christ. She said, "What else *could* I do?" A living body grows.

EVERY MEMBER ACCEPTS EVERY OTHER MEMBER

In the third place, the living body not only feels and grows, but in a living body (now we're getting to a nerve) every member accepts every other member.

I'm a poor carpenter. My wife finally talked me into

hanging a picture. Grasping the nail between thumb and forefinger, I swung the hammer, but hit the wrong nail! Ouch! Imagine the right hand beating on the left, then when the left says, "Ouch," the right shouts, "You stupid idiot! What were you in the way for? I was trying to hit that little piece of metal and you got in the way!" No! The right hand soothed the left. The left thumb went into a sympathetic mouth for comfort.

We all have the same one life in all of us, in Christ. Every member accepts every other member. Each is protective of the other, hurts with the other. "Each considers others better than himself."

The theme of the Ephesian epistle is announced in these words,

> "In the fullness of time, God saw fit to gather together in one all things in Christ which are in heaven, which are on earth, which are under the earth; all things even in Him."*Eph. 3:10*

He wanted us to be *one.*

To the Galatians, Paul wrote, "In Christ there is neither Jew nor Greek, bond nor free, male nor female. We are all one in Christ." For us he could have gone further, "neither black or white, young or old, rich or poor, illiterate or educated, American or foreigner, ad infinitum." We have such difficulty being a fellowship where every member accepts every other member. We are so insensitive to the struggles of new Christians! Our expectation levels are so high!

We expect new Christians to have their hair cut a certain length, their dresses a certain length, "churched" vocabulary, new life-style, even keeping hours similar to ours. Especially we want religious *ritual* already established. If not, we find such difficulty warmly absorbing them into our fellowship. Oh, brothers! *Every member accepts every other member!*

Once in British Columbia I performed the most unusual wedding I've ever seen. There were sixteen people at the wedding; three preachers and one preacher's wife. Eleven people were alcoholics. One of them was on parole (attempted murder of some Mounties, while in a drunken fit). Another one was a prostitute. The groom was 47 years old and the bride was 27 years old. She was expecting a child in two months and they already had one child that was two years old.

Now watch this—every one of them except one was a Christian! That's right, a New Testament Christian! In fact, the bride and groom had been baptized on the preceding Sunday. When Jesus took control of their lives, they changed. This was why they finally decided to get married.

The woman who had often prostituted herself for a case of liquor in the past had by now already led some people to Jesus.

The man on parole, last count I had, baptized six people, whom he had taught himself, with his own hands. Here was a fellowship with no pretenses. They didn't try to "appear righteous to each other. They knew that they were sinners redeemed by the blood of Jesus. The thing that made them different from the old crowd was not their "good track records," but the power, love, grace and mercy of God.

I don't think their sins were any uglier than mine. Different, yes! But uglier? "Every member accepts every other member."

Of course, I don't think these things are becoming to Christian conduct. They are not. These people were *new* Christians, had already made radical changes and had some growing to do. But every member accepts every other member! (Look at the New Testament!)

Look at the people who followed Jesus around. I wonder how many preachers would travel through the country with that crowd tagging along? Tax collector, Mary Magdalene (who some people thought was an ex-prostitute,) Peter, who was a cursing, brawling fisherman, some of those publicans and sinners who were brought to Jesus, as Zacchaeus. Yet they were following Him around, and He wanted them to. *They were His disciples.*

EVERY MEMBER RESPONDS OBEDIENTLY TO THE HEAD

Not only this, in a living body, besides every member accepting every other member, every member also *responds obediently to the head.* We get the picture wrong sometimes. We note that in *Matthew 28:18* Jesus said, "All authority is given unto me." It is easy to place that in *an authoritarian* context where Jesus holds the stick and He is telling us, "line up or else!"

I see the authority of Jesus *in the power of His character* and the *nature of His person.* Once people really saw Him, they could not resist responding to Him. Who is it that has the strongest authority? Is it not the man whom people respect so much that they come to him, confident that whatever advice that he gives will be what they need? People respond to someone like that!

When Jesus spoke, his authority was so compelling that the people were on their way, (some of them to death), in order to do His will.

"All things are put in subjection under his feet." He was given to be "head over all things to the church which is His body." He is in charge of the life of a Christian. *I Peter 3:15* says we ought to sanctify in our hearts Christ as *Lord."* Lord literally means "Master." Our confession is usually, "Do you believe that Jesus Christ is the *Son of God?"* But Paul said, "If you will confess with your mouth Christ *Jesus as Lord,* you will be saved."

Paul said that we ought not be "stupid" or unwise but "understanding what the will of the Lord is." *(Eph. 5:17)* He is in control.

He runs my life because I want Him to. I will respond obediently to the head. I do not necessarily respond to the regimentation of my brethren, even though I am trying to live in harmony with them because I love them too. But my head is Jesus.

I'm not trying to respond to the cultural milieu in which I find myself, even though I must communicate with it. My head is Jesus. The living body responds obediently to the head. If not, it's a spastic body.

THE BODY WITHOUT THE SPIRIT IS DEAD

Finally, the living body feels, the living body grows, in the living body every member accepts every other member, in the living body every member responds obediently to the head, and in the living body, *the body without the spirit is dead.*

I can move; I can think; I can feel; I can walk; I can see; I can speak because I am alive. What's the difference between my body and a corpse lying in a funeral home? All the chemical components are there. It is arranged in an order that it would operate if life were there. But somehow, one lives and one does not. The difference is the *presence of spirit,* the *presence of life,* something we don't even know how to define.

Jesus said, "You are born again." When you were born by that first birth, born of the womb of your mother, you received the life of your parents and the spirit of your parents. The essence of that life is the essence of the-life of one's parents. You gained it by the miracle of birth.

Then he says, "You are *born again;* and your new parent is the Spirit." "That which is born of the flesh is flesh and that which is born of the Spirit is Spirit." *(Jno. 3:3-7)* God's Spirit lives in me and He gives me a new nature. *(Gal. 4:6)* The life that I live in Christ Jesus I live by the power of that Spirit in me. I don't do it by making good resolutions. I don't do it because I've had good upbringing and wonderful training or "strength of character." If I live His way, it's because I am new, because I have a new life-source. And the essence of the new life is the same as the essence of the life of the parent. A body without the Spirit is dead!

"Wooden action" is going on all over the place in churches. I have tried it myself for many years. Brothers and sisters and churches try to live by the power of intellect, will, muscle and "character." "I can do it! I am a competitor. I will keep my mind alert. I am disciplined. I have learned "will power." So, *I will be a Christian!"* No! Never!

No one who is really honest with himself feels this has ever happened. Maybe the will can do some minor "improving." The rest may be covered from the eyes of the brethren, but the real deep sin problem is not solved. The *nature* is not changed. The body without the Spirit is dead! And the church without the Spirit is dead! It doesn't move. It doesn't live. It doesn't breathe.

I wish we could see in our century things happening like they happened in the first century. I'm neither critical nor despondent about the church today. I believe in the Church of the Lord. I think we are in the only situation of any religious group of which I know to effectively and really be the people of God. We are not tangled up in centuries of machinery. Yes, we have unofficial machinery. But we have the freedom, too. And we are committed to a Biblical approach. We have the opportunity to be God's living body here and everywhere. I pray that it can happen.

The living body feels. The living body grows. In the living body every member accepts every other member. In the living body every member responds obediently to the head, because the living body is alive with the Spirit of God, living in it.

Because I believe in the positive power of God, because I believe in the Spirit of God living and working through men, because I think I see in myself and in many other of my brothers and sisters a real hunger to be the church of the Lord, and experience being Christ's body, I believe that wonderful things lie ahead. They may mean that some of the things we have *thought* were sacred will have to go, to make room for things that *are* sacred. But God is *God* and people want to know God. Like Cervantes' *Man of La Mancha,* I see before me a vision of hope, and I want you to dream it with me!

> To dream the impossible dream . . .
> . . . This is my quest,
> To follow that star,
> No matter how hopeless,
> No matter how far.
> To fight for the right,
> Without question or pause,
> To be willing to march into hell
> For a Heavenly cause . . .
>
> . . . And the world will be better for this
> That one man scorned and covered with scars
> Still strove with his last ounce of courage
> To reach the unreachable star.

Right now you can begin reaching for that star simply by saying, "Jesus, I want you to be Lord of my life. I'm surrendering myself totally to your lordship. I am signifying this by going down into your grave in baptism to receive the remission of my sins, to rise and begin walking a new life in You."

WHAT MAN CAN'T DO

We are living in a golden age of scientific advancement. There are amazing things that we take for granted every day, which fifty years ago existed only in the vainest imaginings of wild-eyed dreamers.

For example, a beam of light strikes a face and a voice speaks out in the night. The voice goes silent and the beam of light fades, then a thousand miles and a split second later, in your living room, both spring to life again on the tube of your television set. It's almost a miracle.

Even automobile travel is like sitting in the living room, listening to music, and watching the scenery. It's amazing, isn't it.

Air travel is astounding too. That such a great, huge chunk of metal and all of those people on it would be taken up in the air and carried across the continent in just a few hours, is a technological marvel.

Space travel is more amazing still. And who knows where we're going from here? Who can tell what new worlds may yet be discovered as we smoothly slip beyond the silent stars into new frontiers of stellar space?

No longer are we surprised at a new invention. It looks like man can do just about anything he wants. I said, "It looks like that." But our world is suffering delusions of grandeur. Maybe some Christian people are. We feel that because we have so much power at our disposal, there just isn't any limit to what we can do. We are masters of destiny. We are in control. Consequently, we are missing the main points of life. We skip over the surface like speedboats, rather than running deeply enough to see some of the issues our gadgets can't reach. Even though modern man has stood with some pieces of the moon in his hands, he has never really discovered the peace of heaven in his heart.

MAN IS LIMITED

Man's ability is not limitless. The most significant things, man can't do. Jeremiah said a long time ago, "I know, O Lord, that the way of man is not in himself, that it is not in man who walks to direct his steps."[1]

We don't have the capacity. We lack understanding. We're too weak. We are too sinful.

ONLY THROUGH JESUS

In the first place, *man cannot go to God except by way of Jesus Christ.* We want communion with God. Even people who declare there is no God are probing for some key to life. God created man and took woman from the side of man. We had been one body. Ever since, in the very nature of man and woman, there's a longing to be one. In much the same way, there is something deep within every person that longs for God. Something within us is hungry for a deeper understanding of life, for clearer awareness of the spiritual realities that are around us. Till we find some clue to that, we are lost people.

We long for God. But we cannot go to God. We cannot gain communion with God or access to the blessings of God *except by way of Jesus Christ.*

The Bible says, "And there is salvation in no one else, for there is no other name under heaven given among men by which we must be saved."[2] Only in Jesus.

That's why Jesus said, "I am the way and the truth and the life; no one comes to the Father, but by me."[3]

We try it different ways. We try through our own morality to qualify for God's attention. But God said,

"For by grace you have been saved through faith; and this

is not your own doing, it is the gift of God—not because of works, lest any man should boast."[4]

Sometimes we try to qualify by our own intellect, by our own insights. But the Bible says that even the "foolishness of God is wiser than men, and the weakness of God is stronger than men."[5]

There is only one way man can meet God on common ground, and that's in Jesus Christ. Jesus is God come as far as God can come to meet us. Man must move out of himself, abandon himself and come into Jesus Christ to meet God. There is no other way. While man is capable of many things, to come to God without Christ is something that man just simply cannot do!

COMPLETE HEARTFELT OBEDIENCE

No one can come to God even by way of Jesus Christ without *complete and heartfelt surrender to the will of Christ*. Last Sunday evening a college student said to me, "What is this you mean? You oversimplify this. You say, 'Accept Jesus Christ as your Savior.' That sounds like mental gymnastics. Now, if you talk about living by the values of Christ, I can get my teeth into that."

Of course, when we accept Jesus Christ as the Lord of Life, we are not just making a little statement and that is it. But we are not just talking about "adopting a new set of values" either. We are talking about transformation that comes about in life. If a person goes into a baptistry without surrender into the will of Christ as Lord and controller of life, he goes down a dry sinner and comes up a wet one. That's all. Something basic must happen, back at the center of a man's nature. "Jesus" is not just a word to be said. Jesus must become the whole reason that we live. He must become our *only* hope. He must become also the pattern of life. The way He lived is the way we want to live. The complete surrender to his will must come from the changed heart. How does this happen?

First, we come to understand that he *really lives.* We put our confidence in him and from our hearts confess, "We believe in Jesus." That is the first essential! There is no way we can come to God by way of Jesus Christ if we do not really believe that He is God's son. Jesus said, "You will die in your sins unless you believe that I am he."[6]

Thus, morality, simply following the *ideals* of Jesus will not bring us to God.

Second, trust in Him will lead to *change in the nature of our lives.* That's what Jesus meant. "I tell you, No; but unless you repent you will all likewise perish."[7] Repentance is not just a word we check off and say, "Well, I've done it." Repentance is also back at the roots of life.

Before I come to Jesus my will is saying, "I will live the way *I* want to live. *I* want to be happy. *I* want to be "well-adjusted." *I* want to get along with my neighbors. But I'm going to live *the way I want to live.*" Written into the self-serving life is the law of diminishing returns. We can never be fulfilled that way. And there is no escape from the guilt of our sins.

When we come to Jesus the direction of the will changes one hundred eighty degrees. "I will live the way *He* wants me to live. Whether I am getting along with people, whether I am happy, whether I feel fulfilled, all become secondary. My primary aim will be to follow His will. Then I will be happy, fulfilled and rightly related to others. But these things will be by-products of following Him. They will no longer be my primary objective. This is what repentance means.

UNION WITH JESUS

When the transformation gets this deep, we will be ready to couple ourselves with the life-giving sources of Jesus. We will have come to be ready for baptism.

Three observations about baptism will occupy our attention here. We must not view baptism merely as a church rite to qualify us for membership in the church. It has deep, heartfelt significance.

First, *"Who* is baptized?" Second, *"What* is baptism?" And third, *"Why* are we baptized?"

It really matters *who* is baptized.

It is not just anybody that can be baptized! Only certain people are baptized. They are people who genuinely believe that Jesus is the Son of God. Someone who does not believe, is not ready. A child who does not have the mental capacity for this kind of faith is not ready for baptism. Jesus said, "He who believes and is baptized will be saved."[8]

Peter said, *"Repent* and be baptized."[9]

A *believer* who is willing to *abandon his self-will and his sin* is the person who is ready for baptism.

This indicates the candidate for baptism must be mature enough to comprehend these things. He must feel the pressure of his sins, understand the nature of Jesus' death and be willing to yield himself. He does not have to know everything. But he needs to know that he is lost and that Jesus will save him and how.

Next, *"How* are we baptized?" Like the *who,* the *how* is also important. What the Bible says to this is clear. The years have a way of changing things around. Words sometimes change meaning. The English dictionary defines the word *baptism* in several ways. One definition is "to bury one in water." Another is "to sprinkle water on someone." Another is "a spiritual experience of initiation into a religious community."

But what does God's word mean when it speaks of baptism? In the Bible, baptism is immersion in water.

"And you were buried with him in baptism, in which you

were also raised with him through faith in the working of God, who raised him from the dead."[10]

That we are actually buried is made even clearer in *Romans 6:2-4.*

"How can we who died to sin still live in it? Do you not know that all of us who have been baptized into Christ Jesus were baptized into his death? We were buried therefore with him by baptism into death, so that as Christ was raised from the dead by the glory of the Father, we too might walk in newness of life."

I am wondering how many of us can speak any Greek? There is one Greek word that everyone knows well. The word: "baptism." It is not an English word.

When the King James translation of the New Testament was done, the translators found themselves in a difficult situation. The King who commissioned them to do that translation (and the religious society of that time) believed that baptism was sprinkling. (There is another Greek word for that. That is the word *rantizo.*) But *baptizo* means "to dip, plunge, bury, immerse." So when they came down to the word *"baptismos"* they did not know what to do. If they put "immerse" or "bury" they would be in trouble with the boss. If they put "sprinkle" they would be in trouble with their consciences. So they simply did not translate it. They just left it. It was "anglicized" some: *baptismos* to baptism. (See, you could speak some Greek and did not know it.) The word baptism literally means a dipping or plunging or burying or immersing!

But the beauty of baptism is its symbolism. Remember what it signifies. Remember who the person is that is qualified for baptism. He is a believer who has abandoned himself or has "died to himself."[11] He is crucified. The only thing to do with a dead body is to bury it. He is also seeking union with Jesus Christ. When Jesus had been crucified and was dead, they buried him. People make pilgrimages every year to Palestine to see the place where Jesus was buried.

Carolyn and I have gone into the little cave where it is thought that Jesus was buried. It was a moving experience. But there is a much more real sense in which we can go with Him into the grave. It is when the dead-to-sin man is buried in the waters of baptism. We are "buried *with* Him" in baptism. In that act we come into union with Jesus Christ. And when we are raised up from baptism, "We are raised to walk in newness of life."[1][2]

Theoretical discussion has no real meaning without the concept of *burial.* Death of the old man. Union with Jesus. New life. Coming out of the grave. Born again. "Therefore, if any one is in Christ, he is a new creation; the old has passed away, behold, the new has come."[1][3] That is the *how* of baptism.

Now the *why.* Any sensitive human being is concerned about motive.

This week my wife's dishwasher went out. So I bought her a new dishwasher. I told her it was her Mother's Day present.

"Mother's Day present. She really did not accept it as a Mother's Day present. It was not a tender expression of affection. It was a practical "have to." The motive took it out of the "gift" category. I bought it because the other one went out. (Frankly, I had even forgotten this weekend was Mother's Day.)

We care about motives! When it comes to baptism the motive makes a difference too.

Mid McKnight tells that one day a young man came to his office.

"Are you Mr. McKnight?"

"Yes."

"Are you the minister of this church?"

"Yes."

"Well, I want to be baptized."

Mid had never seen the man before so he said, "Why?"

The man said, "Well, you have the most beautiful church building in town. I want to join this church."

Of course, Mid did not baptize him right then. Sometime later the man came to understand more of what it meant to be committed to the Lord Jesus and he was immersed. But the motive would have been inappropriate if it were merely to "join up with the people that have that nice building."

In Arkansas a few years ago I was preaching in a gospel meeting. A man and his wife were coming every night. As far as I knew, the woman had never yielded her life to the Lord Jesus. The man was a Christian who had let the world pull him away. People were praying for them. They kept sitting a seat further toward the front each night. Well, about the second to the last night of the meeting, when we started to sing the invitation song, the man came forward. He told the people, "I have left the Lord. I have left the church and I want to come back.

Of course, everyone rejoiced. They concentrated their prayers on her. "Will not his wife now become a Christian?"

The next night, lo and behold, when the invitation song began she came forward with tears streaming down her face. She confessed faith in Jesus. She was taken into the baptistry and immersed.

When we went out of the building she said to me, "I want something made real clear. Brother Anderson, I have been a Christian for years. I have always believed in Jesus since I was a little girl. But I want *you* to know that the only reason I was baptized tonight was because my husband and I have always fought over religion, and I've gone ahead and done it his way so we wouldn't fight about it anymore."

My heart was heavy as I drove away from there that night. That woman did not understand the *why* of baptism. I'm glad she wanted to "bury the hatchet." But, I do not think she understood that this meant she was signifying the death of herself and the union with the life-giving source, Jesus Christ. What is the real motive?

Read four passages of scripture. See what you conclude about the motive for baptism. Ask yourself, *"Why baptism?"*

First, *Acts 2:38*. This is when Peter preached the first sermon after the resurrection on the Day of Pentecost. He told the people they had killed the "anointed one." The people were struck by the force of it. They believed him. Their hearts were burning and they said, "What are we going to do?"

Listen to what Peter said, "Repent and be baptized every one of you in the name of Jesus Christ *for the remission of your sins* and *you shall receive the gift of the Holy Spirit."* This is *why!* "For the remission of sins." And, "you will receive the gift of the Holy Spirit."

Let's look at another one—*Acts 22:16*. On this occasion Saul of Tarsus, this young Jewish graduate of the rabbinical schools, a Zealot, an enemy of Christianity, had come to learn that Jesus really was from God. A Christian came to him and told him how to become a Christian and told him about the ministry God had for him. "Why do you wait?" he said. "Rise and be baptized, and *wash away your sins, calling on his name."*[14] Baptism is "to wash away sins."

It is also to "call on the name of the Lord."

Consider yet another passage—*I Peter 3:21*. Peter was making a comparison between initiation into Jesus and the situation back in the days of the flood. "God's patience waited in the days of Noah, during the building of the ark, in which a few, that is, eight persons, were saved through water." And then the figurative comparison—"Baptism, which corresponds to this, now saves you." He added, lest we misunderstand, that the water does not save us. It is Jesus who saves us—at the point of baptism. "Baptism saves you, not as a removal of dirt from the body but as an appeal to God for a clear conscience." It could be translated, "The discussion and settlement of a good conscience with God." We ask for and receive a good conscience in baptism. That is the time that Jesus saves us.

Another reason *why?* "In Christ Jesus you are all sons of God, through faith." Well, how do you become a son of God through faith in Christ Jesus, Paul? The next verse explains, "For as many of you as were baptized into Christ have put on Christ."[15] Baptism is "in order to get *into Christ.*" The original language here is literally, "Baptized into union with Christ." This is how we become one with him. This is how we "plug in" to the source of forgiveness and power which is in Jesus Christ. "Baptized into union with Jesus Christ."

"Do you not know that all of us who have been baptized into Christ Jesus were baptized into his death?"[16] That's baptism.

Another motive is simply "to follow" Jesus. Jesus was baptized. He wants us to follow him.

Now, when you were baptized, if you were baptized, what was the reason for it? Was it simply because some other young people were baptized and you thought it would be a good thing? Was it because you wanted to apply for membership into a religious order? What was the reason? Or, was it the way God wants it to be—a yielding surrender that actually culminates in death with Jesus and resurrection with him.

GOD MUST BE FIRST

We cannot go to God except by way of Jesus Christ. We cannot go by way of Christ without complete and heartfelt surrender to the will of Christ. Not only that, we can't even go that way *unless God has been given first place in our lives.*

We cannot say, "Back there I was 'converted,' and so Lord, you have to admit me to heaven." He wants children who are captivated by His will!

He is not asking for perfection. No! But, I believe that I am saved because God is the one that I want to have first place in my life. That is where the joy comes from. That is where the peace comes from. That is where life begins to make sense. Whenever we try to run life ourselves, whenever we try to put something else before God, nothing fits quite right.

But when God is front and center, things work out right. We discover a moral system that fits. We discover an ethical system that fits. We discover wellsprings of love that give us peace and joy. We discover a sense of cleanness and forgiveness that makes us feel free. We discover a hope that makes us able to meet any crisis in life and defeat it. We discover victory over our sins. He did not promise these things unless the life is yielded. God wanted this in the Old Testament.[17] He wants it still. Jesus is not just Savior, but He is Lord, as well.[18]

PERSONAL RESPONSIBILITY

But there is something else we cannot do. We *cannot repent for someone else.* I cannot give myself to the Lord Jesus for you, and you cannot for me. The Bible says, "We must all appear before the judgement seat of Christ that each one may receive good or evil, according to what he has done in the body."[19] The opposite does not follow. We *can* put stumbling blocks in the way of others. We can create an environment or an example that leads other people to sin.

A certain little boy, the story goes, worshipped his father. (Little boys usually do that.) One morning his father got up, shaved, put on his coat and headed out the front door through the freshly fallen snow. Around the corner, up the block, into the tavern he went. He ordered his glass of poison and was sitting there drinking it. Then he noticed. There on a bar stool next to him sat his little four-year-old boy. He was absolutely horrified. He had never let the boy see him with a drink in his hand before.

He said, "Son, what in the world are you doing here?"

The little boy replied innocently, "Well, Daddy, I just followed your footsteps through the snow."

When you become a parent you begin to feel responsibility.

We do offend others. The way you listen to the preaching of the gospel may be a determining factor to the person sitting next to you. He came looking for hope. If he finds you asleep, he may decide there is no hope here.

Every facet of the life of a Christian may have its effect on someone else. But we cannot repent for the other person.

Many would be glad to go into a baptistry every hour, every day they live, if that would help someone else. I would weep oceans of tears for you, but it would not help you for me to do that. Every person is responsible before God for himself. You are, and I am. Each one of us is.

WE DO NOT KNOW

There is one final thing that we cannot do. *We cannot know the day that God's mercy will cease to be extended to us.* It could happen when the Lord returns.

I thank God that there are times in my "pilgrim's progress of faith" when I am able to say, (and mean it), "Come, Lord Jesus." Yet the human part of me is not really sure he's going to. The faith side says He will. When, we do not know. But the day that this life is over is really the time that God's mercy will have ended for me.

We generally think of death as a morbid subject.

I once preached in Missouri. Wonderful family of Christians there. We had some great high school students. One of the brightest spots was a boy named Ronnie Mills. Ronnie Mills was a super athlete. He could sing. He could just do everything. He thought he wanted to preach the Gospel.

We moved later to British Columbia. We were nearly 3,000 miles away from those kids. But, that first year they kept writing and saying, "Next summer we're going to come and help you tell people about the Lord." One of the parents was going to let them have a Volkswagon bus and they were going to spend the whole summer. I got a letter one day outlining the whole plan. It was from Ronnie Mills.

But before I got the letter I had received a phone call that Ronnie Mills was dead.

If I had made a list of the people in that congregation in the order their deaths would occur, I would have put Ronnie right near the bottom. But he was at the top! We cannot know when God's mercy will be terminated for us. We cannot.

We hunger to go to God, but we cannot go except by the way of Jesus Christ. We cannot do that without yielding with our hearts to His will, so He has first place in life.

We cannot make this decision for someone else. It belongs to us. And now is the only time of which we are assured.

The Lord loves us so much. He is ready to save us right now if we will just come and give ourselves to him. Now that beginning—that *is* something we *can* do.

---

[1] *Jeremiah 10:23.*
[2] *Acts 4:12.*
[3] *John 14:6.*
[4] *Ephesians 2:8-9.*

[5] *I Corinthians 1:25.*
[6] *John 8:24.*
[7] *Luke 13:3.*
[8] *Mark 16:16.*
[9] *Acts 2:38.*
[10] *Colossians 2:12.*
[11] *Galatians 2:20.*
[12] *Romans 6:4.*
[13] *II Corinthians 5:17.*
[14] *Acts 22:16.*
[15] *Galatians 3:26-27.*
[16] *Romans 6:3.*
[17] *Exodus 20:3.*
[18] *Romans 10:9-10.*
[19] *II Corinthians 5:10.*

TASK

THE GOSPEL OUTREACH*

In the opening lines of his vital book *World Aflame,* Billy Graham quotes the reflections of the late Dag Hammarskjold: "I see no hope for permanent world peace. We have tried so hard and we have failed so miserably. Unless the world has a spiritual rebirth within the next few years civilization is doomed."[1]

The perverseness of men without Christ is rapidly breaking through from the spiritual into the more popularly understood dimension of the material. As God is being banished further into His heaven, the building blocks of our world come tumbling down around our ears. Political and social upheaval rock the continent. Large breaks continue to appear in the levees of our moral system as license and perversion threaten to drown decency. As Christ has less control upon us, we have less control of ourselves.

We are being swept into the tense vacuum of empty living. God is cast aside for little gods of materialism, hedonism, intellectualism, and escape.

It falls the task of the church today to reverse this overwhelming trend toward destruction. Our Jesus has the power to "heal the nations." He has done so often before. In a world that would plunge the last glowing embers of faith into the chill waters of secularism we must rekindle His bright flames of commitment and hope.

Against such overwhelming odds, this looks so hopeless. Upon so few, so much depends. "Change Your World" is the name of the game. The stakes are desperately high. And at the moment it does not appear that we are winning.

Yet ours is not a logical time for despair. At no hour in

* Delivered at Abilene Christian University Lectureship, February, 1969.

111

history have God's children had greater tools for the task. The potential for travel and communication is staggering. Many congregations have aggresive and optimistic programs for evangelism. We are employing with telling effect both the literary and the electronic mass media. We are beginning to tap our too long dormant financial capacities. Tomorrow is ours and God's.

In spite of all this however, clouds of disillusionment are settling in many parts of the brotherhood. As one moves among the churches and listens to perceptive preachers, elders, and other astute leaders, he seems to sense an almost universal mood of futility. Maybe it isn't here in this large excited gathering, but it is out there where lonely vigil is kept over the flickering watchfires of faith.

Sensitive and informed men are saying, "We have tried so hard and achieved so little. While we are reaching out so vigorously we are not touching so many areas of genuine need. Some of our most elaborate projects have seen only mediocre results."

Perhaps most disheartening of all is the fact that so few are really involved in the experience of gospel outreach.

Could it be that there is something constructive that will come out of this sense of futility? I cannot help but feel that beyond the shadows we shall see the sun. We are learning something of major importance.

We are being reminded in a new way of the old truth that *method* is not *Gospel.* In the first place, although many techniques of evangelism have been devised, no one of them is universally successful. We must use *all* the weapons in our little arsenal and seek constantly to develop more, but even this is not enough.

Second, all of the technique in the world is superficial without direct, personal, and massive involvement in the vital concerns that rend men's hearts.

Third and above all, we have learned that the spreading flame of Gospel outreach cannot be manufactured by techniques. The Gospel outreach is more than money and machinery and mobilization. These are wonderful tools, but they are only tools. Real evangelism must begin on more primary ground. It is a spreading flame that does not always accompany the sound and fury of publicity. Techniques, equipment, and programs are valuable, but we are beginning to realize we have fastened too many of our hopes to them. Followers of Jesus cannot be "ground out" wholesale. The dynamic of contagious Christianity cannot be simulated electronically, nor by the "hoopla" of organization and promotion. It is a flame that must first be real, God sent, and kindled from within. It will spread most effectively from soul to soul like a forest fire through the tree tops. Its best Public Relations gimmick will be its own obvious worthwhileness in the lives of those who have it. The real power to reach out is a total and devastatingly genuine surrender to the Savior.

The disheartening fact is that this leaves our actual present capacity for real gospel outreach relatively small in comparison with the great throngs that swell our gatherings. There are precious few such authentic specimens of the spirit around.

We *have* thought that didn't matter. If we could find the right gimmick for mass distribution, a skeleton crew could do the job. Having tried that, we now have a growing awareness that souls are still saved one at a time by first hand contact with people whose lives demonstrate the validity of our plea.

When we realize how far we have to go and remember how difficult and slow and individual it is to cultivate genuineness, we become overwhelmed at the immensity of our task. It is long and difficult and not always written in the triumph and excitement of large numbers.

The task of outreach is not for those seeking a comfortable religion. It is a desperately rigorous challenge and it demands the biggest and best within us.

The world cries for something genuine. Outreach is predicated upon the assumption that what we have will really meet men's needs. Before we are ready to reach out therefore, it is imperative that we do some reaching in other directions. First, we must reach up.

FIRST: LOFTY UPREACH

"If ye then be risen with Christ, seek those things which are above, where Christ sitteth on the right hand of God. Set your affections on things above, not on things on the earth."[2]

The word "anthropos" (Greek for man) has buried in its etymology the rich phrase, "the up-looking ones." Something within us must look up or we are less than our best.

One reason we must look up is to establish lines of communication with the Father. We will always be small people no matter what our numerical, intellectual, or financial strength, unless we are a people who are constantly elevated by our vision of the Great "I AM." J. Wallace Hamilton, in his scintillating *Serendipity* gave body to this truth:

"In one of the many art galleries of Europe there is an old Greek statue of Apollo, a beautiful figure of physical perfection. Someone visiting the gallery said he didn't know which was more impressive to him, to look at the statue or to watch the crowd as they looked. Invariably, he said, everyone who stood before it, even for a casual instant, began to straighten up, put back his shoulders stand tall— the lifting power of loftiness.

I think that is what the Bible is mostly about from the beginning to end—little people looking up; people very much like ourselves, who one day look up and see a great thing and then become what they see."[3]

I am always stimulated by a visit with Isaiah. The young prophet looked too low at first. He saw only his illustrious king Uzziah. But when Uzziah died, Isaiah looked up. "I saw the Lord." So transported was he at the majesty of Holiness that the sinfulness of man overwhelmed him.

"Woe is me, for I am undone. I am a man of unclean lips
and I dwell in the midst of a people of unclean lips, for
mine eyes have seen the king the Lord of Hosts."[4]

The purging coal that touched his lips so ignited him that
he could not but share his Holy vision with the "people of
unclean lips." "Here am I send me." This is what God does to
men.

We cannot survive spiritually without daily private
communication with the Father. These golden moments
ought to be an exciting two-way dialogue. Into them must
creep a sense of the magnificent. "How can I close this book
except to pray and then quickly open it again to see what
facet of Him will next break through to astonish me." Power
for gospel outreach is generated in sacred intimate hours of
upreach toward the Father.

We must also reach up to come under absolute captivity
to the Christ. It must be no longer "I that live, but Christ
living in me." We must be powerfully disciplined and
emboldened by the "mind of Christ."

According to a modern parable, a new church building
carried above the pulpit an inscription boldly declaring, "WE
PREACH CHRIST CRUCIFIED." At the side of the pulpit
was a potted creeping vine. It grew up the wall till first the
word "Crucified" was covered and the sign read, "We Preach
Christ." The next word was covered and it read, "We
Preach." Finally the word "Preach" was covered and there
was nothing left but the exclusive little word "We." Churches
can become living sequels to this parable. How often has the
burning zeal to preach Christ crucified been cooled by the
waters of intellectual sophistication. The soul-saving, life-
changing Christ becomes merely a social force and a
humanitarian ideal. It is only a step till Christ is veiled alto-
gether as the unwritten motto becomes just "We Preach."
The sermons get duller with nothing about Christ and quite a

little about politics, philosophy, and psychology. Finally, things degenerate to the word "We" and all that remains is a semi-religious clique rattling around in an old edifice with ladies' tea on Thursday afternoon and men's shuffleboard on Saturday nights. The fire has gone out.

The crucified and risen Christ must have the day or the fires of outreach are quenched before they start. Elton Trueblood in his exciting suggestion that we become an *Incendiary Fellowship* says:

> "Since the starter of the fire is Christ himself, our initial means of achieving a real blaze is that of confronting Him as steadily and as directly as possible. When the closeness to Christ is lost, the fire either goes out or it merely smoulders, like the fires in the great swamps . . . which are hidden from the sun. A Christianity which ceases to be Christ centered may have some other valuable features, but it is usually lacking in power."[5]

Yet so easily when we talk of "The Spirit of Christ," we conjure up vague and emotionally maudlin moods which defy definition. Often they merely amount to whatever religious experience one enjoys most. Jesus of Nazareth is not vague, however, but is a distinctive and winsome reality boldly striding through the New Testament.

This was Paul's soul-winning technique:

> "And I brethren, when I came to you, I came not with excellency of speech or of wisdom, declaring unto you the testimony of God. For I determined not to know anything among you, save Jesus Christ, and Him crucified."[6]

Jesus is the power and Jesus is in the Gospels. Further to this Trueblood says,

> "To confront Christ is really to allow Him to confront us, for we are changed by direct acquaintance. Fortunately this is made possible . . . by the incredibly valuable accounts preserved in the Gospels . . . If any sincere seeker will try the experiment of reading the Gospels for a year, slowly and consecutively, but above all, prayerfully and also with

an open mind, it is practically certain that something of importance will occur in his life. If he stays close enough, for a sufficiently long period, to the central fire, he is likely to be ignited himself."[7]

We must be committed to the startling, captivating man, Jesus. We must also look up to the lofty Son, Immanuel, "The mighty God." And more joyfully still, Christ must be "my personal Saviour." He must be Master to whom every thought is under captivity or we are less than His. To capture every breath of the winds of His compelling spirit the white sails of our voyage must be set. To preach the real Christ without preaching the distinctiveness of His church and obedience to this message is impossible.

In the initial contact, the man on the street is not concerned about our theology, our prestige, or our intellectual prowess. He will watch to see what Christ is doing for us. If he is convinced that the Christ we profess to follow is working for us, it will be easy for him to believe that Christ can change his life also.

SECOND: WARM ACROSS-REACH

Secondly we must reach across.

"Neither pray I for these alone, but for them also which shall believe on me through their word; that they all may be one; as thou, Father, art in me, and I in thee, that they also may be one in us: *that the world may believe that thou hast sent me.*"[8]

Unity is indispensable to evangelism. Before we will become effective in gospel outreach there must be warm links of communication within the brotherhood.

There can be no doubt that the church in the New Testament was an irresistible community of redemptive love. To that self-seeking and ruthless world, how bewildering was the relationship between Christians. The amazement of the pagans is distilled in the exclamation, "Lo, how they love one another."

On the other hand, there can be little doubt that a major hindrance to gospel outreach today is internal fragmentation. Why are we such masters at misunderstanding? What is there in our souls that brilliantly equips us to spot incidentals (such as inept illustrations or slightly deviant opinions), while at the same time we have an amazing capacity to miss massive and vital spiritual truths from one another? Why rather torpedo a brother's usefulness than tolerate his mistakes and listen to his heart? What a barrier this diabolical mentality is to gospel outreach.

Staggering as the task apppears in the face of increasing urbanization, we must be again a family of believers. Warm fellowship has an immeasurable drawing power to souls cast on the cold stones of our impersonal world. What an oasis in the desert of human selfishness and indifference is a body of people where every member accepts every other member, and loves him regardless of status or the color of his skin; where the words, "I love you," "God bless you" and "I am sorry" flow freely.

An early symbol of Christianity was, to many people's surprise, not a cross, but a fish. After the close of the New Testament, the attributes of Christ were reduced to a five word statement: "Jesus-Christ-God-Son-Savior." The first letters of these five words in the Greek form the word ICHTHUS, or "Fish." As persecution began to force the church underground, the sign of the fish became a secret password for Christians. In those dark days something of fellowship was experienced that we need today.

The story goes that a Christian found himself on a lonely desert trail with night approaching. Because the area was infested with robbers and wild beasts it was all a man's life was worth to spend the night there alone. For Christians there was the added hazard of spies of the Caesar against the saints.

Topping a rise the nervous traveler saw across the valley the imposing figure of a rugged, dangerous giant of a man approaching him. Fear and apprehension mounted in the young disciple's heart.

There was no place to flee. Finally he stood face to face with the frightening stranger. Cautiously, with his toe, he drew a rude fish in the dust. The stranger's eyes fell to the fish. Then the light of joy broke across his face and leaping to throw his arms around the young Christian he cried, "Thank God. We are brothers. Tonight we can pray in this place. How fare the saints whence you came?"

We, too must be the across-reaching ones that keep alive and growing a vital communication within the body. Then we can, with more telling power, reach out to rescue the perishing.

THIRD: A DEEP IN-REACH

Thirdly, there must be a deep reach within. To make sure we are ready for effective gospel outreach we must look carefully to our own hearts to assure an expanding capacity to receive sinful men.

The church is a redemptive fellowship. It is not a country club, but a hospital. We must see men's "possibilities, not their perversities."

The gospel performs miracles. God forgives and makes us as pure as if we had never sinned. He assures grace to overcome. But make no mistake about it, the body, the mind and the emotions of men can be so entrenched in sinful living that the process of overcoming the world is not always instantaneous. We must be prepared for great numbers of men with great sins to come into the church. We must be ready to accept such men without reservations and to struggle with them side by side against their sins and our own.

How many new converts are lost for two reasons. First, they are not effectively taught and counselled in the new life and second, because we have not the capacity to accept the weak and "love the sins out of them." According to Matthew's account of the Great Commission, we are commanded to teach men after they are baptized as well as before. "New Converts' Classes" are wonderful and we need more. But it is easy to assume that all of the new converts have the same set of problems and that mass "grounding" in first principles will meet the needs of all individually. I am confident that the discouraging, dominating sins under which a new Christian often struggles will seldom even come to the surface in a large class. If they do, it is impossible to conquer personally tailored sin patterns by group-gained knowledge of the "elemental principles of the Bible." Personal sins demand personal attention—real unqualified caring on the part of those who have learned how to care from the Saviour.

This was crucially illustrated once where I was called to preach a follow-up meeting after a "campaign for Christ." There had been thirty people baptized in the campaign. So, the follow-up meeting was to "mop up the left-overs." When I arrived that first morning there were two groups of people in the vestibule of the building. Here were the *"mature* Christians," and over there were the *"new* Christians." I think only six or seven new Christians were there three months after thirty had been baptized.

There was a strange atmosphere. Some of these new disciples had come from some rather problematic backgrounds. One of the older Christians confided, "We don't know just how to handle this thing. You know in these campaigns they get taught rather quickly, and we're not very selective about the ones we approach. We don't really know how deeply converted these people are. So we're *just sort of watching to see if their commitment proves to be stable before we absorb them into the ongoing program of the Church."*

Frankly, I was angry. I wanted to say, "Man, don't you see what you are doing? Who would take a newly born baby out to the edge of town, leave him with a pile of diapers, several bottles and a gallon of milk and say, 'All right son, I'm going to come back in three weeks to see how you are doing. If you show any inclination that you want to stay in the human race, we'll take you home and let you live with us.'" No! The weakness and helplessness of the infant must be understood. He must be nourished and taught and loved. The same is true of the infant Christian.

If we are not ready to receive the suffering from the world, there is no point in gospel outreach. We are not in any position to win a world for Christ unless we are ready to receive that world into redemptive healing fellowship.

Lofty upreach is vital, and warm across reach and a deep reach within to make room for the lost. There are three dimensions of height, breadth and depth which are indispensable to "the outreaching ones." Then we are ready for the gospel outreach.

FINALLY: GENUINE OUTREACH

When all is said and done, Jesus still says, "Go."

Someone recently pointed out to me that the "Go" of the Great Commission is not an imperative command but an assumption. It assumes that the Christian will be moving about among men. Where he goes, what he does will be optional, but not his sense of mission. His life must be outreach.

The "Go" does involve three imperatives, however. In the first place, gospel outreach demands *Approximation*. We must go where people are. Although our church buildings are wonderful tools, in some ways they are profound hindrances. They have a tendency to lull us into the delusion that attendance at the church building is the vital substance of Christian living; that what goes on there is "religious" and the rest of life is "secular." This comfortably isolates us from the lost. Distant cries from polished pulpits will not save men on the other side of the brick and mortar barriers. There must be contact.

I shall never forget the day my father took me to the train when I left for college. I am an only son. He knew I would never live in his house again. He set my cardboard suitcase on the platform and nervously began pumping my hand. He tried to talk, but no words could come. Then he put his arm around my shoulders, then back to the hand, over and over. Finally he muttered, "Be strong, son," and turned his face away. I know he drove home with a heavy heart that day.

But did you ever stop to think what it was like the day the Son of God left home? It was time for God to reach out for us. He did not do it by some remote mass-media campaign from a comfortable office in the east wing of heaven. He sent His only son. "The word became flesh and dwelt among us." There must have been heaviness in heaven; the Son hesitating at the door; the Father looking down into blackness, moving his hand in a farewell long after the Son disappeared, in His eyes the shadow of the cross. Why? Even God could not announce the terms of the gospel by distance. Jesus had to leave home and come down to where men wept and laughed and worked and played and sinned and prayed and lived and died.

We must leave home too. We must go. There can be no substitute for going where the people are.

The second imperative in the "Go" of Gospel outreach is *Penetration.* We must penetrate every phase of our world. We must touch men as they are mid-stride in the functions of Twentieth Century living. Vitally equipped disciples, ignited with the flame of Gospel penetration must be found at the nerve center of men's needs: in the laboratory, factory, office, grocery store, government, and university. This, not as an escape to less demanding religion, but as a courageous thrust into the strategic forefront of Faith's frontiers. Dispelled must be the crippling myth that the height of spirituality is to be a preacher and that somehow the Christian who has secular employment is less Christian than the "full-time minister." All must be full-time ministers, each seeking a stratum of humanity to which he can bring the Christ.

A third imperative in the "Go" of the gospel outreach is the word *Reconciliation.* There is no hope in the world if we seek only to "Christianize society" or to "Evangelize the institutions of man." It is not the primary task of Christians to educate men out of the slums, to protest race and class inequalities, or to equalize standards of affluence, although these are concerns that we cannot ignore. Ours is a vastly larger mission.

We plead, "Be ye reconciled to God." The New Birth, the revolutionizing of individual men by the dynamic of the revolutionary gospel, is the crux of our calling. Men are lost, for time and eternity, without Christ. We cannot afford to forget that even for a moment.

Christianity is a taught religion. It is best taught soul upon soul, where its power in the teacher can become contagious in the learner. "God was in Christ, reconciling the world unto Himself . . . and hath committed unto us the word of reconciliation." And how do we do it? The same way the Son of God did it.

How did God do it? When He got ready to reconcile the world to Himself, he did not just shout over the back porch of heaven. He sent Jesus, not only into our world, but into our hearts. The "blood of His cross" was saying poignantly, "I love you and I want you to come home."

It is our task now. Can we expect more than God? We cannot shout over the ramparts of our fortresses with the Saviour's message for His estranged loved ones. We must go into men's hearts, calling them back to God.

> I said, "Let me walk in the fields,"
> ' He said, "No, walk in the town."
> I said, "But there are no flowers there."
> He said, "No flowers, but a crown."
> I said, "But the sky is black,
> and there is nothing but noise and din."

He wept as he sent me back,
"There is more," He said, "There is sin."
I said, "But the air is thick,
and clouds are veiling the sun."
He whispered, "Yet souls are sick,
lost, in the dark, undone."
I said, "But I'll miss the light
and friends will miss me, they say."
He said, "You must choose tonight
whether I am to miss you or they."
I pleaded for time to be given.
He said, "Is it hard to decide.
It will not seem hard in heaven
to have followed the steps of your guide."
So I took one last look at the fields
Then I set my face to the town.
He said, "My child do you yield?
Will you trade the flowers for the crown?"
Then into His hand went mine,
And into my heart came He.
And I walk in a light divine
A path I had feared to see.

—Author Unknown

---

[1] Graham, Billy, *World Aflame,* (New York, Garden City: Doubleday and Co. Inc., 1955), p. 1.

[2] See *Colossians 3:1-2* KJV.

[3] Hamilton, J. Wallace, *Serendipity,* (Westwood, New Jersey: Fleming H. Revell Co., 1965), pp. 47-48.

[4] See *Isaiah 6:5* KJV.

[5] Trueblood, Elton, *The Incendiary Fellowship,* (New York, Evanston and London: Harper and Row Publishers, 1967), p. 115.

[6] See *I Corinthians 2:1-2* KJV.

[7] See Trueblood, Elton, *op. cit.,* p. 115.

[8] See *John 17:20-21* KJV.

BRINGING RECONCILIATION TO ALL MEN*

Knowlton Nash, reporter for the Canadian Broadcasting Corporation, described a dramatic incident the third week of July, 1966. His plane was approaching Detroit Air Terminal. The intercom crackled to life. The pilot dipped the left wing and said, "If you look now you will see the saddest sight in America." It was what seemed a whole city aflame. The rough edges of two races grated together in the early stages of the "riot syndrome" which has become the hallmark of a decade.

This is but a small sample of the extent to which world community is torn into fragments. Years ago George Eliot said, "We are islands isolated from each other, shouting lies and threats across a sea of misunderstanding." Today it is only more acute. There is the Generation Gap, domestically. The Student Revolutionary Movement has spilled from the campus to the street. Color, class and creedal confrontations rock the continent. Cultural and political incompatibilities combine in a complex global convulsion.

When we have telstar and intercontinental jet service, why do we have so many communications breakdowns?

At least in part, this fragmentation results from our lack of inner purpose and our loss of destiny. While technology has enabled us to stand with some pieces of the moon in our hands, we still don't have the peace of heaven in our hearts.

Gone are the days when most men rose from their beds with the first blush of dawn, prayed before breakfast and then grasped the plow handles with a sense of meaning. Gone are the nights when, weary from productive labor, they pillowed their heads with the deep assurance, "Fear God and keep His commandments for this is the whole duty of man."[1] As we dash aimlessy about, we bump into each

* Delivered at Herald of Truth Workshop, June, 1967.

125

other's territories, prejudices and ideals. That is why in a shrinking world we are feeling all around us the jagged edges of fragmented man.

OUR PURPOSE

Who will "heal the nations?" Technology tried: Marconi let us hear each other. The Wright brothers enabled us to visit each other. But we still don't understand each other.

The economists have said, "Spread the wealth and all shall eat. Security is the key." But the hunger is too deep to be banished with bread.

Education said, "Men must learn." But rather than learning to communicate, we have only learned to increase the complexity of our problems. Education is not salvation.

It falls the task of the church of the Lord today to draw these fragments together into one "new humanity." "By abolishing in his flesh the law of commandments and ordinances, that he might create in himself one new man in place of the two, so making peace."[2]

Our mission is putting men together properly so that the world will come out better. God's word states it this way:

> "All this is from God, who through Christ reconciled us to himself and gave us the ministry of reconciliation; that is, in Christ God was reconciling the world to himself, not counting their trespasses against them, and entrusting to us the message of reconciliation. So we are ambassadors for Christ, God making his appeal through us. We beseech you on behalf of Christ, be reconciled to God."[3]

Alienation between men results out of man's alienation from God. We are separated from God because " . . . your iniquities have made a separation between you and your God . . . "[4] That is why Christ is so universally appealing. He heals the *source* of our sorrows.

"What attracted the people in the Roman Empire, first the slaves and the lower classes, but soon men of highest education? Why did they join, at the risk of their lives, the despised and forbidden 'sect' of the Christians? Because it offered to them what no other religion, not even the synagogue, could offer: the forgiveness of their sins in the name of Him who had loved each of them so that He even died for them."[5]

It is *not* the primary task of Christians to educate men out of the slums, to forge legislation that will remove race and class inequities in all nations. These may be noble goals, but we have an infinitely more serious mission. We are ambassadors, pleading, "Be ye reconciled to God, and this will reconcile you to one another!"

We often fall beneath our majestic purpose. We are failing to *touch* many of the fragments with the word, let alone to blend men together. Why? To such a complex question there is no simple answer. However, think on these factors. We are failing to communicate the Christ, at least partly, because we have unwittingly limited Him at home and tarnished His cause abroad *by identifying Him with special interest groups.*

The gospel of Christ was not designed for just one segment of mankind. "There is neither Jew nor Greek, there is neither slave nor free, there is neither male nor female; for you are all one in Christ Jesus."[6] Wherever men are won to the Christ, barriers will fall. "For in Christ Jesus you are all sons of God, through faith."[7]

Sons of the same Father are brothers of each other—a world family!

When God got ready to reconcile the world to Himself, He did not do it by some remote mass-media campaign from a comfortable office in the east wing of heaven. He sent His only son *into our world.* "God was in Christ reconciling the world to Himself."

We cannot shout over the ramparts of our fortresses. Yet sometimes we try!

First, we are often found shouting over the ramparts of *middle class "respectability."* In our domestic mission thrust at home the appeal is sometimes limited to other people much like ourselves—white, middle-class, Anglo-Saxons. By this we miss large segments of the North American lost. Not all are white. Not all are middle-class.

A massive segment of the leadership of God's movement is in air conditioned isolation, dresses in neat middle-class suits and shiny shoes. I wonder what this says to the Puerto Rican in New York City's slums, the black in the ghetto, the bearded Berkleian or the blue-collar in the factory complex? Do they want what we have? Maybe! But we are from another world of which they are both envious and suspicious.

Second, in our mission abroad, we are found to be shouting over the ramparts of *North American culture.* To allow the church of our Lord to become identified with assumed Western "superiority" is to defeat our purposes. Jesus did not cling to any one nation. His gospel does not prefer any particular form of government. Our flags get in His way.

There is a wonderful tingle in the pit of the stomach and a deep feeling of clean gratitude when "Old Glory" dances against blue sky to the strains of "America." However, it may come as a shock that this often has a reverse effect outside the United States.

It is so easy to assume that the trappings of Western culture are part of Christianity. It is also an easy assumption that the American way of life is desirable to all people. Few are convinced that Christianity and American ideals are even compatible. American viewpoints, political or otherwise, injected into a message beamed into other countries can often intensify rather than diminish the fragmentation of humanity.

OUR PROBLEM

The word of the living God is the only power to heal broken humanity. Our challenge, then, is to find how best to communicate the word to all facets of the race so that it will be accepted as relevant. Like Jesus, we must "leave home," not just geographically, but psychologically, culturally and nationalistically.

This means *first* that we will seek to understand others' points of view. The late Pandit Nehru of India said,

> "If we seek to understand a people, we have to try to put ourselves . . . in that particular historical and cultural background . . . We have to understand their way of life and approach. If we wish to convince them, we have to use their language as far as we can, not the language in the narrow sense of the word, but *the language of the mind.*"[8]

The apostle Paul said it this way, "I have become all things to all men, that I might by all means save some." [9]

Second, if we would heal broken fragments of humanity across national lines we must divorce the gospel from Americanism. Not only must the externals of our *presentation* to other countries be free from the artifacts of America, we must also guard the *content* of the message, making sure that we are not confusing the everlasting and universal gospel with the trivia of American political and cultural tradition.

Other countries must not be made to feel the "downward slant" as if they were the unenlightened, receiving light from big paternal North America. All nations regard their own culture as superior to the rest. They do not need to borrow, or even to appreciate our culture, but they desperately need Christ!

Christianity has not existed to support civilization, but civilization has existed for Christianity's larger growth. Grasping this concept would save us from the notion that our way of life is the last word and that it is the business of religion to support and preserve it. The New Testament gospel was not subservient to any nation or system. It was the way of God for the ages, *the way to which every system and every nation must adjust* or die.

OUR POWER

Jesus has power to heal the nations. He has done so often before. He was out to win a world. He might have said, "I am the light of Galilee," but he said, "I am the light of the world."[10]

He might have said, "God so loved the Jews," but he said, "God so loved the world."[11]

Let us not disguise Him in an "Uncle Sam" hat or a "grey flannel suit."

He does not rise or fall with class, creed, color or culture. He transcends and outlasts such trivia.

Christ has seen the rise and fall of several social orders, political systems and economic complexes, but He lives on. Amid the ruins of each of the grandest of human dreams he keeps saying, "I am the way."[12] When men turned to Him He welded them together into a " ... kingdom that shall never be destroyed ... "[13]

"Peace on earth, good will toward men," is what the angels said. Did it happen? Yes! Among *some* men. Those who hated one another before Jesus came later knelt together, ate together and sang together. Government officials were one with slaves, publicans and harlots as they shared tears with theologians. Fishermen sat down with kings. It can happen today, too. It does when we let Christ be the universal "Prince of Peace."

It was somewhere in the heart of what is now France that a Roman soldier was sent on a strange mission. He was told to take forty young Christians out to a frozen lake in the dead of winter, strip them of their clothing and send them naked onto the wind-swept ice. Should they renounce Jesus and call Caesar "God" they could have their clothing and their freedom.

The forty young followers of Jesus went courageously into the bitter night. The soldier drew his heavy robe around him and began his awful vigil. The mournful wind carried across the ice sounds of voices, singing:

> Forty wrestlers, wrestling for Thee, O God, Claim for Thee the victory and ask of Thee the crown.

"What is it," he mused, "That could make these men sing into the teeth of death. Oh, yes, I know the story about the man from Galilee. I have heard how, when He *passed* by, whole villages would follow Him into the desert just to hear him. The deaf, they say, heard, the blind saw and those who had not smiled in years laughed openly for joy and returned home with songs in their hearts . . . =They say, too, that He *was executed,* but that God made Him live again, and that He *still lives.* His followers do not fear death nor each other; Jews and Gentiles have ceased cursing and have begun embracing one another . . . "

The song was heard again, only this time it was changed. He chilled. "*Thirty-nine* wrestlers for Thee, O God . . . "

"Oh, no! Did one of them die out there?" he thought.

About that time came a wretched specimen of humanity crawling to the fire. "Give me my clothes or I die. I will renounce Jesus, I will call Caesar 'God' . . . anything."

By this time the soldier had heard too much. He threw down his robe saying, "Here, take mine." He dashed off into the wind shouting, "I would rather die with your Jesus than live with my Caesar."

Soon the song came back full strength again, *"Forty wrestlers,* wrestling for thee, O God, claim for thee the victory and ask of thee the crown." He was one with his brothers on the ice.

"He hath given to us the ministry of reconciliation." Keep clear the lines of communication. Ring loud the call, "I pray you in Christ's stead, be ye reconciled to God."

[1] *Ecclesiastes 12:13.*
[2] *Ephesians 2:15.*
[3] *II Corinthians 5:18-20.*
[4] *Isaiah 59:2.*
[5] Sasse, Hermann. "Sin and Forgiveness in the Modern World," *Christianity Today,* March 3, 1967, pg. 5.
[6] *Galatians 3:28.*
[7] *Galatians 3:26.*
[8] Jawaharal Nehru. *Visit to America,* (New York: John Day Company, 1950), pp. 58-59.
[9] *I Corinthians 9:22.*
[10] *John 8:12.*
[11] *John 3:16.*
[12] *John 14:6.*
[13] *Daniel 2:44.*

FRIENDSHIP EVANGELISM

The offices of the White Star Lines in Liverpool, England were jammed with frantic people. Few moved their eyes from the huge board high on the wall. The "unsinkable" Titanic had just sunk in the icy waters of the North Atlantic. Names of those rescued or known dead were being posted on the board. There were only two columns, "saved" and "lost".

When the eyes of God look at the world He sees us in similar terms. Two categories: "Saved" and "lost". His heart yearns over us.

He wants our hearts drawn into His compassion. He wants us, like Jesus, "seeking the lost". Through His message He would be continually moving names from the lost column to the saved column. If we will be faithful messengers!

The soul-winning imperative must never be forgotten or ignored. Our mission is clear: "To seek and to save that which is lost".

Few Christians have forgotten. Only at great pain of conscience would many ignore. But in spite of this, as a fellowship, our evangelistic picture is dim.

Why? Who can unravel all of the complexities of one human heart, much less understand with precision the motives of a whole brotherhood? However, let me suggest some possible problems and a possible angle of approach to solution.

SOME PROBLEMS

Some feel evangelism is *for a specialized people—* the evangelists. Thus because they may not be talented as public— proclaimers, they see soul winning beyond their capabilities. True, not all have been given the "gift" of evangelism in that specialized sense of the term.

The church has one *mission.* It has many related and supportive *ministries.* The Lord has given each Christian a gift or gifts to fulfill some special ministry or ministries within the body.

To illustrate: If my family drives to Canada, our *mission* is to get to Canada. But many *ministries* are involved in the trip, which contribute to its meaningfulness and aid in achieving its goal. We must stop for gas. Children will need the rest room. Drivers will relieve each other. We will need rest. We will need to eat. Each family member will have some unique but important contribution to make to the overall joy and success of the venture. That is using gifts for ministry. In turn ministry is being supportive of mission.

But, we could circle the block here in Abilene exercising our gifts on the same ministries—and never get to Canada. The *ministry* would be meaningless if the *mission* were forgotten.

In the church our mission is seeking the lost. Bringing them into saving relationship with Jesus and into vital life-giving relationship with His church. To the Ephesians Paul wrote, "He gave *some* evangelists." To others he gave other gifts for varying ministries. Not all are expected to be "evangelists" in the specialized sense. But, for the mission of the church to be accomplished all "gifts" must definitely in some way aid our mission. Each must share the gospel in his own way—not just by the priceless example of Godly living, but by the actual word of mouth message!

Others are evangelistically paralyzed because they see evangelism only in terms of *one specialized method*—be it door knocking or bus ministry or "cottage classes": People are inclined to see soul-winning in terms of one method familiar to their congregation. And if they don't feel competent in that area or don't feel suited to that kind of relationship—the sharing of the gospel looks like a good thing, but *impossible* for them personally. Not only will their gifts be lost, but the person himself will likely be plagued with guilt feelings.

We must see our sharing of the gospel in more natural terms. We must not bring pressure upon people to join the "personal work program: if this implies—"do it this way or you are not doing it". We must see that there are as many evangelistic models as there are people and situations. We must see that not everyone can lead a lost person all the way from A to Z, from lost to saved. In fact God may have given a specific Christian the gift and task of bringing some person only *one inch* of a *thousand-mile journey* toward the Lord. But we must be used for that one inch or a lost soul may be one-inch short of our God-given mission to Him.

Numerous Christians feel incapable of evangelism because they see it as *a task only for the "learned".* Some of this feeling may result from a misperception of *I Peter 3:15,* "Always be prepared to make a defense to any one who calls you to account for the hope that is in you, yet do it with gentleness and reverence."

Have you ever said, "I would try to share the gospel if I knew enough answers, but I don't. So I am afraid to try. I better leave it to someone who is "ready to give an answer". Peter is not saying "be equipped to explain every minute theological point one might raise. Not even everything the church stands for or that you personally believe in. Peter's point is: "Stand willing to share what you know of the Lord and what hope he has set blooming in your heart."

Rather than evangelism being a specialized task for a skilled communicator and astute theologian, it is the natural sharing of every Christian, in whatever way his abilities and circumstances best suit him. And it is the sharing of meaningful and precious things he has already experienced through Jesus.

FRIENDSHIP EVANGELISM DEFINED

Sometime back John R. W. Stott was being interviewed by a national TV personality. Stott, an Episcopalian, is an unusually clear and helpful Biblical expositor. He was asked, "What do you think about evangelism?"

Stott explained that there were some kinds of evangelism which were personally distasteful to him. He spoke of the guilt-motivated, "button-holing" of strangers, designed to press gospel fragments upon them.

"But," he said, "I am turning more and more to what I call "friendship evangelism". I liked his term. What did he mean by friendship evangelism? I suppose it could be illustrated this way: I like to hunt. If a person is my friend, and he likes to hunt, and I know where there is a bargain sale on shotgun shells it is natural for me to tell him. On the other hand, I don't stop many strangers on the street to discuss the price of ammunition with them. I have never confronted a stranger on the plane to tell him where shotgun shells were cheapest.

Yet, most of my hunting *friends* know. Why? Because it is natural for friends to know each other's interests and to share that which is of mutual benefit.

This is "friendship evangelism". Sharing of matters of mutual value and concern with a friend. So, share, brother! Share what you have with your friends, and make more friends for more sharing. Not all must be "missionaries" to the strangers.

Of course "sharing" assumes you *have something* to share. This is why Peter *begins* by saying, "First sanctify in your heart, Christ as Lord". *Then,* and only then will you be "ready to give a reason for the hope that is in you".[1] After all superficial excuses for evasion of evangelism have been offered, we must confront the real problem: Frequently it is that we have nothing to share. No message!

Not that we don't care that someone is lost. We do. But we have nothing vital and life-changing to offer him, because Jesus has not be "sanctified in *our* hearts" as Lord.

You may reply, "Oh, but I do believe in Jesus." But the question is "is he really set apart (sanctified) as Lord in your heart?"

The word sanctify means "set apart" or "special, other different". This same word is used in a different form for the English expression "holy". Holy, meaning totally other! The priest, for example, was a sanctified (holy) man, because he was "set apart" for a special function. A saint (all Christians are saints) is set apart completely for the Master's use.

When Peter said, "Sanctify Jesus in your heart as Lord" it was strong medicine. He meant make sure that in your heart there is *nothing at all like Jesus.* No one occupies such a special position. Your heart is His. He will brook no rivals.

STRANGER EVANGELISM

Now, when we *know* Him and He is set apart in the holy places of our hearts, things will be different. Will we have a guilt-ridden compulsion to button-hole strangers on the streets and say "You are lost"?

I would call this "stranger evangelism". There is an urgent need for getting the message to strangers. This can be done by the print and electronic media. It can be done through campaigns and campus confrontations or what-have-you. It was done in Biblical times. It needs to be done now.

However, the purpose of stranger confronting and media evangelism is not to do the total task of change. It is best suited primarily to surface the people whose hearts are ready. It can do this. But it is limited. It certainly won't have the same warmth, power and credibility as can personal conversations with people we know and with whom we regularly interface. It is needed, but compared to friendship evangelism, it is often too wide of the mark, too shallow in content and too weak in impact and appeal. Also, not every Christian is gifted for "stranger evangelism."

FRIENDSHIP EVANGELISM'S APPEAL

Now let us look more closely at "friendship evangelism" and its power and appeal. We approach the matter in six steps:

First: *We must have a message!* That message cannot be a speal we have learned. It must be the reality of Christ being sanctified in our hearts.

We have church houses full of people who have never felt enough need to do anything except be baptized and go to church so that they will be good "church members". Until we have come to feel broken, to hurt badly enough, that no human being can meet our needs, we will likely not find and accept a life-giving message. We cannot merely "recommend church", inviting our friends to come and sit on a pew a couple hours a week, hoping against hope they won't find it as distasteful as we have. We must tell our friends about the Lord. How he can specifically bless them in places they hurt because he has blessed us in places where we are hurting. Then we are beginning to "sanctify Christ in our hearts". Then we will be better equipped to "give reason for our hope" and in doing so stimulate hope in others.

That is friendship evangelism. Is there anyone who cannot do that. It doesn't take intellect. It doesn't take winning personality. It doesn't take salesmanship. If you can read, you can underline. Underline the passage that has spoken to a specific need in your life. Dog-ear the page where your underlined passage is located, to know where in the Bible you have received that blessing. Know so you can share it with someone else who hurts in the same place.

Second, *you must have a friend.* This is not just a surface, social acquaintance. We need to reach out for real relationships. Be patient. Love much. Serve faithfully. Listen long. Share freely. Be vulnerable.

It is not just a gimmick to be open and vulnerable. Let us freely acknowledge our own blind spots. Let us create a climate of trust, respect and concern until finally the friend can really and genuinely and vulnerably reveal his true self to us.

Third, *we must begin with his felt need.*

It is a common mistake for us to be answering questions that people are not asking. To deal with valuable truths of the gospel before the person is ready to hear them is of little value. To keep this from happening we must know what need the friend feels. We must wait and be open enough for him to reveal his true need. When we speak directly to the "sin problem" (and we know of course the real problem is sin) the person may not hear us because he does not feel like a sinner. He does not see the cause-effect relationship between his felt needs and his alienation from God. He does not understand that his loneliness, or meaninglessness, or tension, or fear, etc., are actually rooted in sin. So we must be careful not to be impatient.

Let's wait and listen and watch. Pray to be sensitive to his "felt" needs.

If we come on directly too soon and say, "You are lost and you need the Lord". Communication may fail. The response may be, "Lost? I know where I am. This is 16th Street."

He doesn't know what we are talking about.

"No, I think you are going to hell."

"Hey, man, why are you cursing at me?"

"No, I mean you need your sins forgiven."

"Sins? What sins? What is this sin thing?"

We may be speaking in one language and he is hearing in another. Why? We are not relating to his *felt* needs. Again, Why? Because we don't even *know* his felt need. We are too busy talking to his *actual* needs, before he is ready for that.

Remember baseball? You were in a batting slump. Three games in a row; nine strike outs in a row. So you told your friend, "I have this problem. Everytime I get up to bat I freeze up. Maybe my stance is wrong?"

He says, "Have you eaten banana pudding?"

You say, "Or maybe I am choking up on the bat too much?"

He says, "With peanut butter on it?"

You have a *need*. He has *something good*. But they don't appear to you to be related to each other.

This often happens when we "stranger evangelize".

But when we are near the felt need, the door is open. And anyone can go through it. All we know is, "I hurt. Brother I hurt. Right here. And I have discovered the goodness of God on that point."

Maybe at church the preacher pointed out the passage that spoke directly to my need. I underlined it and dog-eared the page. I read it again on Monday. I said, "Isn't it good? The Lord knows me!"

Possibly it could have been something as simple as Psalms 103:14:

"For he knows our frame; he remembers that we are dust."

Isn't it good to know that God knows how frail and ordinary we feel, but still loves and accepts. And something deep in the heart says, "Thank you Lord for that."

Then, lo and behold, my friend is talking. Out tumbles one of his inner hurts—his "felt needs". If we love and wait they will.

The friend may say, for example, "I messed up at work again today. Got the books so fouled up I'll have to work overtime five evenings to correct it."

Here is an opportunity! We can say, "You know what? I have felt the same thing. I hurt."

Most of us, if we have walked very far with Jesus, have hurt in enough places and found enough blessings from God to touch those places, that we will rarely run into any new hurts.

So I can say, "But God helped me." And I can flop open my Bible to that dog-eared spot and read the underlined verse.

"The Lord knows my frame is dust!"

See! God understands. God knows bank tellers foul up occasionally."

My friend says, "You mean God knows me? God cares that I had an imbalance in my accounts today? That's really something!"

And I can say, "Yes!"

That's friendship evangelism.

Now, is the person a Christian because he knows God understands about tellers fouling up the books? Of course not. But now we have his interest. Now we have begun to relate what God is saying to a real point in the friend's felt need.

Fourth, *we build credibility for the word.* That is we keep repeating this process.

As we stay around friends we discover more and more of their needs. We find more opportunities to tell what the Lord says to those "felt" needs. We will find his confidence, in the Lord and His word, growing. We are no longer talking banana pudding to a batting slump. We are showing him what God says about the felt need in his life.

But remember. We cannot do this if we have not gone to the Lord ourselves, never carried our needs to him and to his book. Thus we will need to have "tasted that the Lord is gracious" and that he can fill our own needs, before we have the resources to "friendship evangelize".

If we have been underlining and dog-earing, when a friend reveals a hurt we can simply un-"dog-ear" and say here is what God says to that. Gradually we are leading this person to a greater confidence in the Lord and in his word and we are developing in him a holy hunger and a Christ curiosity.

Fifth, *they must finally be confronted with the Gospel.* When the trust relationship has developed more fully, and the person's confidence in the word is obvious, we will finally need to clinch things. We will need to turn from the areas of "felt" need to "real" need; the root cause. We will finally gently and lovingly tell the person that the real source of his problem is sin and alienation from God. We will tell him that the only way is the cross. Then we will show him the way of God's grace through faith, repentance and baptism. We will explain death to self, Lordship, and other such basic concepts. This *must* finally come or we have not been a real "friend".

Sixth, *we will by this time have made this friend to be friends with our other friends.* Some of these will be

Christians who are members of the congregation where we are. So already we will be miles toward drawing this new baby Christian into a live and meaningful relationship with the church. He will already belong in the circle of friendship, which through acquaintance with the Lord, will now come to have deepened and richer dimensions. This will diminish new-convert losses which seem to plague every evangelistic thrust.

Now hopefully, the new Christian will naturally imitate the way in which we have related to him. He will naturally share the gospel through "friendship evangelism" as it defines itself in *his* gifts, personality, and circumstances.

EFFECTIVENESS OF FRIENDSHIP EVANGELISM

Some of the favorable aspects of this form of evangelism are obvious.

In the First place, *anyone can do it.* It is not for specialized people. It fits everyone's circumstances of life on some level and in some form.

Second, it is *much more natural to deal with real issues.* To try to indoctrinate a stranger is much more difficult than to share real spiritual events in our lives and real meaningful passages with our friends.

Thirdly, probably most important of all is the fact that *friendship evangelism is a giant step toward solving the "drop- out" problem.* We are concerned that people become members of the church with enthusiasm, and then soon fade away. Often they have genuinely been baptized into union with Jesus. They have seen warm and enthusiastic assemblies. But when it comes to real relationships with the people in the church it seems there is no way they can crack the circle. It is usually not that anyone is consciously trying to exclude them. It is just that there is no convenient "plugging-in place" for them. It just happens. They are not drawn into the circle.

Bobby and Diane Green are some of the loveliest Christians in the Highland Church. They are just now a little over a year old in the Lord. They had no difficulty becoming involved in spite of the size of this congregation. Reason? Betty and Alton Davis had loved them for a long time. They had waited until their need was looking for an answer and they spoke God's answer into it. And when they came to church they didn't have to look for friends. They were already going to church where their best friends were. Betty and Alton Davis and their circle of friends were already the circle of friends of Bobby and Diane Green. That meant that for them friendship evangelism certainly helped to overcome the involvement-dropout barrier.

COSTS OF FRIENDSHIP EVANGELISM

Let us sound a warning here: Friendship evangelism is costly! There are some special risks. I mention three of these specifically:

In the first place, it is costly *to befriend the unlovely.*

The urgency of our task and the principles of good stewardship demand that we first share the gospel with the person who is most likely to receive it. We can be bad stewards of our evangelistic energy. Often we spend weeks, months, sometimes even years, trying to convert someone who is already very religious. We feel more comfortable with people that are somewhat like us already.

I am not trying to imply that because someone is religious everything is o. k. I am saying that the hardest person in the world to get to admit a need for the Lord Jesus is someone who already thinks he has the Lord Jesus.

The most obvious target of evangelism is the person who is totally unchurched, totally uncommitted, and whose lifestyle is totally unattractive to Christians. These people may be hard to befriend, but once befriended, easy to teach. There is no hard line of religious prejudice. There is no pall of security already draped over them.

It is difficult for me as a middle-class American to befriend the person who most needs the gospel. I would rather protect myself, surround myself totally with church people, at least surround myself with good upright religious folks of the community.

But for friendship evangelism to succeed, I will need to befriend the person who will receive the gospel. He may be a very unlovely person.

This unlovely person may even present a threat to me. Not just that he is distasteful for my "Christian sensitivities." It may be that his life-style presents temptations that ordinarily would not be mine. This is a risk I must be willing to take. God took this risk when he sent his son into the world. Jesus took this risk when he left the loveliness of heaven to befriend the unloveliness of earth. He was even accused of being tainted himself because he was the friend of publicans and sinners. But even though we are not "of the world" we must be "in the world". Paul said that he had become all things to all men and that by all means he might win some.

A second cost is the *risk we run of losing meaningful and valuable relationships.* What do I mean? Well, when I button-hole a stranger it may do some good. Some people have a gift for it. Most people don't. (Possibly some who think they have the gift for it are really just working off a fit of evangelistic conscience.) Lots of people have been saved that way. More often however the direct button-hole approach to a stranger is met with rejection.

There is nothing wrong with being rejected for Jesus sake. But when I tell a total stranger, "You need the Lord". And he tells me, "Get lost". What have I lost? I had no relationship with that person to begin with.

Possibly this is why it is easier to campaign in distant cities than to do soul winning at home. If I embarass myself there I can come back home and will have lost no face.

But friendship evangelism is risky. I am talking to my friends. I need those friends. Broken relationships are painful. So when I finally come to a place where I open that dog eared-page and confront my friend with his *real* need, my friend may reject me! If my friend rejects me, I have lost something precious. That hurts. That is the risk.

But again our heavenly father took his risks in his gigantic friendship evangelism attempt. Jesus came down my road and met me. His eyes looked into my eyes. He walked with me for awhile until I believed he understood me. But when he went to the cross he died at total risk. He didn't have one convert guaranteed. Everyone could have rejected him. If "evangelism" was risky for Jesus, will it be without risk for us?

A third cost of friendship evangelism is its *vulnerability*.

When I talk to a stranger, I can lay nice words on him. He doesn't know if there is a dichotomy between my message and my life. And I could easily deceive him.

But when I am talking with my friend, he knows me through and through. There is no way to snow him. So the life of the soul winner must be genuine to be effective. Our honest struggle to cling to the cross must be obvious to that person.

If a friend should call me a hypocrite, the only honest thing I can say is, "I am sorry. Please help me."

By some definitions, that is what we all are. There is a great difference between what we want to be, and what we really are. But you see, we are *trying* and *trusting*. The Lord even accepts those who honestly confess they are hypocritical and struggling to be genuine. We can't hide this from our friends.

We can and we must be honest about this struggle. "Don't look at me, look at Jesus," must be our intent.

The scriptures declare the Christian life to be a life of stumbling and struggle.

FRIENDSHIP EVANGELISM ON A BROADER BASE

Sometime ago I spoke at a Methodist youth seminar. High school and college people from all over Texas were there. The topic assigned was "Witnessing: Blessing or Burden?"

Someone asked, *"How* do you share?" I told them in essence what I have said in the previous portion of this message about "friendship evangelism: and *I Peter 3:15.*

Then someone asked, *"What* do you share?"

"What do you say to people to bring them from lost to saved condition? What is the *message* you give them?"

Now folks in the Church of Christ and folks over at the Methodist Church have a different story on that point. Frankly, I was uncomfortable.

Everyone had a Bible and seemed to respect it. So I suggested that we simply should go to the Bible for our answers.

One student rather innocently asked, "Is there an account in the Bible of people "witnessing" that tells what they said and what happened?"

I said, "Come to think of it, there is. It is called the book of Acts!!!"

So we went to Acts 8. Everyone enjoyed the story of the Ethiopian riding in his chariot. One girl was reading, "he began at this scripture and preached unto him Jesus."

I interrupted, "What happened?"

Answer: "He witnessed about Jesus."

Someone else corrected, "No, he witnessed *out of the scriptures* about Jesus!"

Another chimed in, "We must use the Bible in witnessing. If we don't we are liable to tell only *our feelings* rather than *God's message.*"

I was elated at the insights.

Then someone read further. "They came to a certain water, the eunuch said, "Here is water, what keeps me from being baptized?"

One student asked, "Why did he bring up baptism?"

Another answered, "It must be obvious that when you preach Jesus, people just naturally want to be baptized."

I said, "Hey, that's right."

Finally one of the youth ministers present in the room said, "I didn't know anyone else witnessed that way. Everytime I tell someone about the Lord Jesus, I tell them about baptism. Do you?"

I said, "Man, yes, if I get the opportunity to."

There was an ominious silence for a few moments, then:

"Well, what about the people who aren't baptized then? I am not baptized; am I lost?" It was not a challenge, but a serious self-reflection.

Now I was really feeling pressure. My answer:

"Now you have me out of my depth. The Lord has given me the ministry to preach the gospel. He did not call me to determine people's eternal destiny."

"If you want to know what to tell people in order to give them the message of the Lord Jesus, that part is clear.

Why not leave the judging to God but make sure *we* are faithful to the word in our *message.*"

So we all agreed that it might be a good thing just to begin telling people what the Lord said and what the Lord had done to make their lives better. Then when we have their attention and confidence, to read to that person from the Bible the message of conversion, to tell people specifically to believe, repent and be baptized. These conclusions were reached by the group themselves. I scarcely had said a word.

You see, when the climate is right, and the hearts are right, there will be no need to argue with people. We just share. We share what the Lord has *done* and what the Lord *says.* It is best to avoid speculation. His task for us? "Sanctify in our hearts Christ as Lord, and give a reason for the hope that is in us."[2]

CONCLUSION

Brother, I know about the reason for my hope. I was broken and lost and enslaved by my own ego, by self protection and by self pursuits. I was miserable. I could no longer stand myself, or other people, or God. While I could scarcely bare to live like that, I didn't even have enough courage to blow my brains out and escape it all.

Then the good news began to come through. "The Lord is not willing that any should perish."[3] "God so loved the world," became a personal message to me. It was not "the world" he was loving then, it was Lynn Anderson.

"By grace you are saved through faith, that not of yourselves it is a gift of God and it is not of works lest any man should boast."[4]

I cannot begin to explain the enormous sense of burden lifted. It was like being raised from death to life! My heart was singing, "I can be saved! God knows my name and loves me in spite of myself!"

It is no trouble sharing that with anyone.

His word said, "Quit worshipping yourself. That's what is making you miserable!"[5]

So I said, "Lord, I'll get out of that!"

He said, "I want you to be baptized. Then your sins will be forgiven and you will be filled with the Holy Spirit."[6]

My heart said, "I'll not argue with that Lord." I have tasted that the Lord is gracious. How could that be hard to tell.

If you hurt, you may be deceived. You may think your hurt is because you don't have a good personality or because you're married to the wrong person or that you are not married at all. It may seem to you that it is because you have too many children or that you don't have enough. You may think it is because of your job or any one of a thousand other ideas about why you are not fulfilled. You may think these things are the sources of your problem.

Please understand, they are only the "felt" need. They are the symptom of something deeper. Fact is, you are living in a world in which *you* are the center. Jesus said, "If anyone will come after me let him deny himself, take up his cross and follow me."[7] It's that simple. That's not hard to share is it? The "real" reason for unhappiness is that you are not in fellowship with the Lord Jesus. He is the way to life.

I wish every brother and sister could see that and share that. That's friendship evangelism.

Francis Schaeffer said, "If I have an hour with a man on an airplane, I will listen to him for forty-five minutes to let him tell me his need, then I'll spend fifteen minutes to tell him about the Lord."

If the message is live, if the friend is real, if the time is right, fifteen minutes is ample time to share your hope and the reason for it.

May God speed the day when we see evangelism in its proper perspective. The church has one mission. It has many ministries. Not all have the gift of evangelism. But all must evangelize by using whatever gift they have to be supportive of the great mission of the great body of the Lord Jesus Christ.

---

[1] American Standard Version, *I Peter 3:15.*
[2] *I Peter 3:15.*
[3] *II Peter 3:9.*
[4] *Ephesians 2:8-9.*
[5] *James 4:1-4.*
[6] *Acts 2:38-39.*
[7] *Matthew 16:24.*

STRENGTH

HOPE*

I am inclined to believe what I read recently in one of those pat paperbacks on do-it-yourself psychology: The writer looked into the psyche of a newborn child and said, "Unless a baby has an inborn hope and confidence that his innermost needs will be satisfied, he will die."

Sometimes, that means physically dead, like the poet, John Berryman, who wrote, "I don't think I will sing anymore" and then jumped to his death from a bridge.

Others choose to live physically but are really *dead* like mannequins in the show window of an empty universe.

It is precisely at this point that we see a major distinction between the Christian and the man without God— *HOPE!*

The Bible talks so much about hope. But, when this assignment was given me, after scouring my files I found that out of more than seventeen years of preaching I had *not* one shred of notes on "hope." A four hour conference with a Bible faculty Ph.D. and panic phone calls to two preachers and a competent Christian counselor turned up no additional *lecture fodder* on "hope." So, it seems that while most Christians regularly verbalize the word "hope," we have little concrete knowledge of its meaning. Maybe this is why we frequently feel its absence so much.

HOPE! Faith, Hope, Love—these three—but, what is this "Hope?"

Secular substitutes for hope are easily borrowed by the Christian. One is a sort of tentative desire with little real expectation. "I hope it doesn't rain tomorrow." Understood

* Delivered at Lubbock Christian College Lectureship, October, 1973.

155

in such a shallow sense, hope that should be "the anchor of the soul" becomes a vague, doubtful wish.

Norman Vincent Peale has borrowed, "for religion," another secular concept of "hope": "Think positively. Be confident. Have Hope!"

While this may be an improvement on vague doubt, it still is only humanly generated. It works fairly well when the birds are singing and the basal metabolism is high. But on Friday afternoons and Monday mornings, it is a bit thin.

The writers of the New Testament had something much bigger in mind when they talked of "hope." It was not humanly generated but God-given, and founded, not on the loveliness of the environment, but on the resurrection of Jesus Christ. Hope does not say "perhaps the promises of God may be true; it is the confident expectation that they cannot be anything else but true."[1]

HOPE IS NOT ALL FUTURISTIC

It would be easy to take a short step from here to Resurrection morning, but to do so we might miss something. The Christian "hope" is not simply looking forward to Heaven. Of course, one dimension of our hope is future oriented; this is clear in *Romans 8:24b, 25:*

> "Now hope that is seen is not hope. For who hopes for what he sees? But if we hope for what we do not see, we wait for it with patience."

We will talk of this later.

But, first another dimension of hope begs our attention. Hope has implications for the present. Hope in the believer replaces the despair of the unbeliever. This sense of "being," of aliveness, may be the dominant treatment of "hope" in the New Testament.

HOPE AS SALVATION

"For in this hope were we saved."[2]

One level on which the term "salvation" links with "hope" is our *confidence of safety in the world.*

> "He delivered us from so deadly a peril, and he will deliver us; on him we have set our hope that he will deliver us again."[3]

Notice! This doesn't mean we trust God to always shelter us from danger and trouble, but that He will give us a sense of independence from them—a divine indifference to circumstance.

Another level on which salvation and hope meet is in the rescue of ourselves from ourselves.

When we operate independently of God, we are incapable of managing ourselves.

> "For the mind that is set on the flesh is hostile to God; it does not submit to God's law, indeed it cannot; and those who are in the flesh cannot please God."[4]

When we are incapable of managing ourselves, we ourselves create the source of our greatest unhappiness.

> "I do not understand my own actions. For I do not do what I want, but I do the very thing I hate . . . Wretched man that I am! Who will deliver me from this body of death?"[5]

So, we are, each one, ourself's worst enemy. But that vicious circle can be broken.

> "We know that our old self was crucified with him so that the sinful body might be destroyed, and we might no longer be enslaved to sin."[6]

When we accept, by faith, God's promise that the victory

has already been won in the New Birth, hope is born as well.

If we try to fight sin in hand to hand combat, we are sure to lose. Brooding over our frailties will surely bring despair. But "hope" comes when we look in the right direction. Augustine said, "Look away from yourself; look to God." The Godward look is the key to hope. "If then you have been raised with Christ, seek the things that are above."[7]

When it is not any longer my awareness of my "me-ness" but a hunger for His "He-ness" things are different.

Dr. John Baillie says,

> "At the heart of religion lies the significant paradox, that it is only by coming to care more about God than either about our own character or our own destiny that either our character can be transformed or our destiny in any wise foretokened. The transference of attention from self to God is the secret, both of self-conquest and of hope!"[8]

Then, of course, there is the obvious "hope" in *salvation from the guilt of sin.* "There is therefore now no condemnation for those who are in Christ Jesus."[9] And the hopefulness of this hope is in knowing that forgiveness comes of *His grace,* not of my deservedness.

> "For by grace you have been saved through faith; and this is not your doing, it is the gift of God—not because of works, lest any man should boast."[10]

> "The man who knows Christ can never again despair about himself or his world. He has discovered what Cavour called "the sense of the possible," for he has discovered that "all things are possible with God."[11]

HOPE AS WORTH

It is not uncommon for people to have a "low self-image." For many, the sense of self-worth and personhood appears to have been irretrievably misplaced. Christian hope is the opposite of this kind of despair.

When I know God, I come to see who I am. I am "created in His image." I am "His child."

> "For you did not receive the spirit of slavery to fall back into fear, but you have received the spirit of sonship. When we cry, "Abba! Father!" it is the Spirit himself bearing witness with our spirit that we are children of God, and if children, then heirs, heirs of God and fellow heirs with Christ, provided we suffer with him in order that we may also be glorified with him."[1] [2]

That means I really am "somebody." The *sense of personhood* restored to me by relationship with God gives "hope."

Some time ago, a young woman sat in our living room. She had come to pour out her feeling of non-personhood. She felt rejected by her family. She had become a Christian and for years struggled on alone. Then, she had fallen into sin. She felt guilt-ridden and dirty. Her fiance had abandoned her. She was crushed with this shock. She came to me from the hospital where she was recovering from a second suicide attempt.

She said she was afraid to go home for fear she would destroy herself. She even said, "I can see absolutely no reason to live. I am worth nothing to anyone. If God really loves me, then surely He wouldn't care if I kill myself."

At almost that moment, my three-year-old son bounced around the corner. When their eyes met, a smile of pure sunshine broke across her face and everything in her responded to him, reached for him. Of course, he beamed back at her.

Then came the spark of "hope"! I said, "There's no way I could tell you how much I love that little boy. He is mine. You just made him smile; and I appreciate anyone who brings richer happiness to my son. Now, God has hundreds of children all over the world. He loves them more than I could ever love my son. He wants them happy. He has given you— each of us—a unique way to make his children smile."

"If you destroy yourself, you will destroy a reflection of God, Himself, and you will rob some of His children of the smile God sent them through you."

Several days later, still depressed but doing much better she said, "I think I will make it now—I am *somebody!* I don't feel like a non-person. I have *hope!"*

Because she had caught a glimpse of the "Godness" in herself, she had hope.

HOPE AS MEANING

If the gospel is to engage the world at a point of real, felt need, it will have to speak to *meaning.* Much of the disorder and immoral excess of our day may well be symptomatic of the hollow feeling of meaninglessness. Stripped of meaning, a man will do all kinds of things to contrive the illusion of it, at whatever expense—from burning himself out at business to bending his mind on pills. Few people can live without a sense of meaning. It may be to such a condition that Paul alludes with the words, " ... having no hope and without God in the world."[13]

Some years ago, I was a part of a panel of resource people at a high school symposium on drug abuse. On my left sat three high school seniors, articulate and intelligent—but very much a part of the drug scene. All three spoke openly of repeated experiences with hallucinogenics. On my right sat a pharmacist and a lawyer.

The lawyer expounded the legal penalties for drug abuse. The pharmacist explained physical and emotional risks involved. The three students made their replies. The audience sat in stony silence.

Since I was "resource," it seemed that I should say something, but I didn't know what it should be. Finally, it struck me that we had never discussed the central issue . . . *"Why* do people take drugs anyway? Knowing the legal, physical and psychological risks, why would anyone deliberately and repeatedly abuse himself with drugs?"

Turning to one of the students on my left, I asked, "Why do you do drugs?"

At first he stared at me in mock surprise. Then he said, "Man, you gotta be bombed out of your birdie. It's the end, the livin' ultimate. Doing drugs is where the whole thing is at!"

I couldn't argue with his logic. I told the audience, "That sounds like the right reason to me. If it is the ultimate human experience, if it is the most fulfilling thing you know, if it is working out the ultimate purpose for which you are designed, then, of course, you ought to do it! Don't let legal or physical or psychological hazards stand in your way—if it is the ultimate!"

Then, I explained that I felt the young man had settled for too small an "ultimate." There is an *ultimate* for life infinitely better than hallucinogenics. Not a *thing*. He is a person! He *didn't* live. He *does* live. He is alive in my own life now. And because He is, I know who I am, and I have a sense of purpose and meaning. Life is going somewhere. I told them that I was not afraid to die but that I was not afraid to live either!

I went on to recommend Jesus to the students. I said, "You might not 'buy' Him, but make your decision intelligently. Check the facts. If then, you still reject Him, just make sure you come up with an ultimate that is a whole lot better."

To my astonishment, at this point the audience *broke into applause!* In a plain, old pagan high school! Not that they believed in Jesus, but they were saying, "You are right! We don't know where we are going or what we are here for." But then a point of real insight came.

The lawyer stepped over to me after the program and said, "Look, I'm going to level with you. I am an atheist! But I'm not going to knock what you said to those kids. *Everyone needs a crutch!*" After a few seconds of silent prayer, I said, "Perhaps you are right. Maybe we do need crutches." Then looking him squarely in the eyes–and as earnestly as I could, I asked him, "What is your crutch?"

His face dropped. He shuffled his feet and cleared his throat a time or two, then he looked me back in the eye–struck by the force of the thoughts we were sharing. He said, "Well, I stay real busy."

I think at that moment we both stood on the rim, staring into the yawning canyon of his despair. This is the despair which is the opposite of Christian "hope." The "hope that does not disappoint us."[14] "God is reality! To turn away from Him is to turn away from reality. To turn away from reality is to court despair."[15] But, God is the "God of all hope."

Through Jesus I have become part of the purposes of God.

"We know that in everything God works for good with those who love him, who are called according to his purpose."[16]

Now my presence on this planet makes sense. *Meaning is given to me.* I have hope!

THE RESURRECTION HOPE

Hope is now. But it is also futuristic. As the caption says, "all of this . . . and heaven too!" Here it is in scripture:

"Blessed be the God and Father of our Lord Jesus Christ!

By His great mercy we have been born anew to a living hope through the resurrection of Jesus Christ from the dead, and to an inheritance which is imperishable, undefiled, and unfading, kept in heaven for you, who by God's power are guarded through faith for a salvation ready to be revealed in the last time."[1 7]

Recently a professional counsellor told me that one of the first questions he asks troubled people is "What are your goals, aims, and aspirations?" More than 80% of extremely troubled people have none!

The Christian is on his way to Heaven! That's where he is going! And on the way, he is walking with God.

Yet, to know where we are going is not to imply that we will be able to see everything clearly along the way.

Hope is not in knowing what lies ahead. "What does God want?" we ask. "Give me a blueprint for my life and I'll find 'hope'!" No! Not hope! Boredom and profound disappointment.

M. L. Haskins writes:

"I said to the man who stood at the Gate of the Year, 'Give me a light that I may see my way into the unknown.' And he replied, 'Put you hand into the hand of God, that shall be to you better than a light and safer than a known way.'"

"Hope" is not in ourselves. Neither is it for ourselves. Neither is "hope" in our circumstances. Satan leads us to think that if we had the *things* we want in life, peace would come and hope. If the single were married, the poor rich, the ugly beautiful, etc. there would be happiness. These are false "hopes." For the excitement of the pursuit of pleasure dissolves in the emptiness of achievement. But Christian hope "fades not away."[1 8]

"The anchor of the soul, both sure and steadfast" is not oblivious of circumstance, but it is *above* circumstances and feelings.

In fact, "hope" hits its apex at rock bottom when we find circumstances most painful and confusing. This is why Paul writes:

> "We rejoice in our sufferings, knowing that suffering produces endurance, and endurance produces character, and character produces hope, and hope does not disappoint us."[19]

This Christian "hope" is not the kind that says on a sunny day, "Isn't God good!" Rather it "sings songs in the night."

> "At no time does God love his children's singing so well as when they give a serenade of praise under his window when he has hidden his face from them, and will not appear to them at all. "Ah," says God, "That is true faith, that can make them sing praises when I will not look at them."[20]

Is this what the Psalm means, "Weeping may tarry for the night but joy comes in the morning"?[21]

> "Sing, Christian, for singing pleases God.
> Sing because it will cheer you.
> Sing because it will cheer your companion.
> There is some broken spirit, it may be,
> that will be bound up by your sonnets.
> Sing! Wash your face in a bath of praises."[22]

Let the believer baptize the powerful words of the poet with Christian meaning and sing:

> "Morning has broken
>   Like the first morning.
> Blackbird has spoken
>   Like the first bird.
> Praise with elation
>   Praise every morning
> God's recreation of
>   The first day."[23]

[1] Barclay, William, *More New Testament Words,* Harper & Brothers: p. 46.
[2] *Romans 8:24.*
[3] *II Cor. 1:10.*
[4] *Romans 8:7-8.*
[5] *Romans 7:15,24.*
[6] *Romans 6:6.*
[7] *Colossians 3:1.*
[8] Baille, John, *And Life Everlasting,* (New York: Scribner, 1933), p. 189.
[9] *Romans 8:1.*
[10] *Ephesians 2:8-9.*
[11] Barclay, William, *More New Testament Words,* (Harper Brothers), p. 45.
[12] *Romans 8:15-17.*
[13] *Ephesians 2:12.*
[14] *Romans 5:5.*
[15] Moule, C. F. D., The Meaning of Hope, (Philadelphia: Fortress), p. 28.
[16] *Romans 8:28.*
[17] *I Peter 1:3-5.*
[18] *I Peter 1:25.*
[19] *Romans 5:3-4.*
[20] Spurgeon, Charles H., "Song In The Night," *Decision,* August 1973.
[21] *Psalms 30:5.*
[22] Spurgeon, Charles H., "Song In The Night," *Decision,* August 1973.
[23] Stevens, Cat, "Morning Has Broken."

THE ALABASTER BOX

"There they made him a supper; Martha served, and Lazarus was one of those at table with him.[3] Mary took a pound of costly ointment of pure nard and anointed the feet of Jesus and wiped his feet with her hair; and the house was filled with the fragrance of the ointment.[4] But Judas Iscariot, one of his disciples (he was to betray him), said,[5] "Why was this ointment not sold for three hundred denarii and given to the poor?" This he said, not that he cared for the poor but because he was a thief, and as he had the money box he used to take what was put into it.[7] Jesus said, "Let her alone, let her keep it for the day of my burial. The poor you always have with you, but you do not always have me."*John 12:2-8.*

It was a beautiful little box. Made of white marble from the west of Egypt, it was called *"alabaster."*

The contents were even more beautiful. It contained rose-red perfume imported, at great care and expense, from far-off India. The fragrance was called *spikenard.*

This small alabaster jar of spikenard was used to convey one of God's most beautiful lessons.

The event took place at the house of Simon, a leper that Jesus had cleansed. Several people were there that day. Four faces stand out from the crowd:

FOUR FAMOUS CHARACTERS

Lazarus was there—the man whom Jesus had recently raised from the dead. *Mary,* Lazarus' sister was there. She was a person to whom loving seemed to have been as natural as breathing. Her eyes may well have glowed with love for Jesus. Her heart doubtless ached with gratitude because He had given back her brother from the grave. *Judas Iscariot* was there, the man who betrayed Jesus. And, of course, *the Master* was there.

What a strang gathering. Lazarus who had just been dead. Jesus who would soon be dead. Judas who betrayed Him. Mary who loved Him.

A discussion arose over the following incident: Mary broke the seal on the box of spikenard. She anointed Jesus' head and foot, then dried his feet with her hair. Judas Iscariot bitterly bemoaned the fact that the expensive perfume (worth about $30.00) had been wasted. To him, it was a foolish, worthless impulse.

Jesus stepped into the conversation to rebuke Judas and commend Mary.

THE WAY THREE PEOPLE SAW IT

Three different attitudes toward the alabaster box of ointment appear. The attitudes of Judas, of Mary, and of Jesus. Let us look at these one by one.

JUDAS' VIEW

Jusas Iscariot is a controversial man. One almost wonders how such a rascal could blunder into the companionship of Jesus. It was no blunder. Jesus had *chosen* Judas! But Judas also made some choices. The Bible says that he was the man who kept the purse of community money owned by Jesus and his disciples. It also says he was a thief.*(Jno. 12:6)*

The temptation appears to have been too much for Judas. His character crumbled. *First,* he may have been loyal. *Next,* he was likely along for the ride, hoping that Jesus would become king. In this event, he would be on the inside track with those who shared the big "rip-off."

Possibly, he had totally lost faith in Jesus at this time and was just getting everything he could before he abandoned the Lord's company.

At any rate, by now his conscience permitted him to betray Jesus for a pittance—*and that with a kiss.*

When the alabaster box was opened, he uncoiled on Mary. He *pretended* to be distressed that this expensive ointment had not been sold and the money given to the poor. But he wasn't concerned about the poor. He was greedy. He wanted this money for Judas.

Good motives on the part of other people seemed beyond his comprehension. Judas (like thousands since) was so pre-occupied with himself that it didn't seem possible for one to love enough to pour out such expensive ointment on an impulse of affection. (Makes one wonder about those who consistently find ulterior motives in good things people do!)

This is significant today. We are often afraid to act lest we misuse the Lord's money. In all of the Bible, Judas Iscariot is the only man who was concerned about "saving the Lord's money."

It is to be expected that, to those who are not Christians, honest generosity on the part of Christians looks like foolish waste. More disturbing by far, is to see *Christians* lamenting the *cost* of expressions of love to God!!!

Not long ago a lady was commenting to me on a book that she had recently read. It was the account of five American missionaries who were killed some years ago in Equador—struck down by the savage spears of the Aucas Indians whom they were trying to reach; a magnificent example of total commitment to loving service. This lady's disheartening and insensitive comment was, "What a waste of good young lives!" Jesus has said that this business of living for him may be this expensive![1]

Possibly John's words would have meaning here:

"Stop loving this evil world and all that it offers you, for when you love these things you show that you do not really love God;[16] for all these worldly things, these evil desires— the craze for sex, the ambition to buy everything that appeals to you, and the pride that comes from wealth and

importance—these are not from God. They are from this
evil world itself.[17] And this world is fading away, and these
evil, forbidden things will go with it, but whoever keeps
doing the will of God will live forever."[2]

MARY'S VIEW

Let us examine a radically different view of the alabaster
box from that of Judas. What did it look like to Mary?
Remember, she was a personal friend of Jesus. Apparently he
rested often in the home of Mary, Martha and Lazarus. Mary
by nature loved. She loved Jesus deeply. Possibly, this very
day her mind repeatedly went back to the memory of Jesus
standing only a few days earlier at the tomb of her brother.
She could see again the sobs of grief convulse his great
shoulders. She could see the hot tears of sympathy stream
down his face; for "Jesus wept."[3]

One other thing she could see. Mary seemed to be aware
that Jesus was shortly to die. Though Jesus had mentioned
this often to the others, it did not seem to sink in. Each
person was too absorbed with his own role in the coming
kingdom. *Mary alone understood.*

What a glow there must have been in her eyes that day.
How her loving gaze must have hung first on her blood
brother—joy pounding at her temples. "He is alive!"

Then her eloquent eyes might well have followed Jesus
while he moved around the room—adoration and joy and
sadness mingled in her heart. "He is soon to die!"

What else could a heart like hers do but break the
alabaster box? To her the perfume was saying, "Nothing is
too good for Jesus."

Do you suppose Mary sat calculating the price of that
alabaster jar—debating whether it would be foolish to splurge
it on sentimentality? No! Not for a moment. She loved its
fragrance—loved it even more because it would be a fitting
expression of her heart. *Nothing is too good for Jesus!*

What of my heart? Is it searching itself for something lovely enough, costly enough within me to be a worthy gift for Jesus? We so easily squander our real inner valuables on self interest, feeling the cost is too great to "waste on religion." Hear it, brothers! Jesus is all or he is nothing at all!

The story is told of a woman who said, "I want my son to be a doctor; if he can't hack that, then a pharmacist; if he can't make pharmacy, maybe he can teach high school—but if he hasn't enough brains for that, then I hope he will become a *preacher.*"

This, I hope, is meant to be somewhat humorous. However, I once sat talking with the mother of a young preacher. She said, "I always have felt sorry for him. He always wanted to fly—have a career in the Air Force, but he was rejected on medical grounds—grounded for life." "His second choice," she sighed, "was the ministry."

Something deep inside me was crying. No one should preach as second choice. Where is the spirit of the alabaster box. The best is for Jesus. That goes for any ministry laid at His feet, from bottle-washer to brain surgeon.

We are not immune to this kind of thinking in other areas. I have known people who complained about the cost of the church buildings, while at the same time they lived in luxurious houses. Willing to see the gathering place of the saints a drab cracker-box. Willing to allow crowded, ill-equipped, gloomy "holes in the wall" to pass for Sunday school classrooms where children's attitudes toward church and God are molded. Why? For fear of wasting money! While thick carpet, split-levels, twin autos, and more surround us at home.

Brothers, nothing is too good for the Lord. The tools which we use to teach about Him publicly ought to be every bit as pleasant and commodious as the houses in which we live and teach about Him more intimately. We cannot afford to forget the *real* reason Judas didn't want to break the alabaster box.

The best I can find within me—the most precious, the most beautiful and fragrant is what must be my token of love.

"And so, dear brothers, I plead with you to give your bodies to God. Let them be a living sacrifice, holy—the kind he can accept. When you think of what he has done for you, is this too much to ask?[2] Don't copy the behavior and customs of this world, but be a new and different person with a fresh newness in all you do and think. Then you will learn from your own experience how his ways will really satisfy you."[3]

A poor woman and her daughter attended a mission lectureship. Their hearts were torn by the need. They wept because they had no money to help. They went home in stony silence. They talked into the long hours of several nights. They prayed. And then they penned this short letter.

"I have no money to bear up the hands of the missionaries. So I am breaking my alabaster box. My daughter is the most precious gift I have. I freely give her as she freely gives herself."

Would you lay such a precious gift at the feet of Jesus? Would I? May God grant it!

JESUS' VIEW

A third person expressed views about the alabaster box. It was *Jesus*. Jesus knew the heart of Judas. He knew the heart of Mary. He loved them both. He seemed deeply moved by this extravagant token of love. His attitude is summed up in His words, "She hath done what she could."

Judas bruised Mary. The cheapening of her lovely act on his traitor-lips, twisting her motives, scorning her sacred and private devotion, must have been a blow to the gentle soul of this sister.

Jesus, however, did not leave her long in pain.

"Let her alone," he said, "She hath wrought a good work in me." I would like to do something someday where I could hear Jesus say that to me . . . "a good work." He commended her!

Oh, how it must have moved Jesus that Mary was the only one who loved deeply enough to be aware of his coming death. "She is anointing my body for the burial." What a way of setting a gravestone—of building a memorial.

Men are not even certain today where Jesus was buried, but they still remember this memorial. Jesus said, "Where e'er this goes through the whole world, it will be spoken as a memorial." Mammoth tombs, temples, and mausoleums may crumble into the dust and be forgotten—but the fragrance of the alabaster box has filled the whole world.

THE NATURE OF LOVE

Love can accept individual differences of expression, if they come from the heart. This, too, was precious to Jesus. Just think. Pouring a bottle of perfume over someone! Unwise and useless, you say? Maybe so. That's what Judas said. But who can measure what it meant to Jesus!!!

My children sometime come running to me, filled with sunshine and joy. They have a picture they have drawn, just for me, planning it for love. These pictures will never be sold for commercial value, nor decorate the walls of the London Art gallery. But they are more precious to me than Rembrandt originals. They are expressions of love.

"She hath done what she could"—she loved—and what greater gift is there than that. Lord help us all to love like this—to say "for me to live is Christ, but to die is gain." May the Lord grant also, the grace to be able to receive love, even crudely contrived or impractically extravagant.

Oh Lord, help me break my alabaster box of love and to know you receive it with joy.

WHERE SHALL I BREAK THE BOX

Where shall I break it? I can start at *home*. Sometimes wives like the literal bottle of perfume, not necessarily an alabaster jar of spikenard, but perhaps a glass bottle of "White Shoulders" or "Chanel No. 5" may mean as much. Maybe don an apron and wield a dishtowel. A man will never genuinely love anyone unless he loves in his home.

Let me boast. Did you know that my wife was once in the Miss America contest? In fact, she was a winner. I personally elected her to that status in 1957 and she has won every year since.

She knows, however, that not every day does my Miss America get an alabaster box of spikenard. Sometimes it's a viol of vitriol. But love must begin with those to whom we are the closest.

It will spread into our relationship within *the church*. Have you broken an alabaster box of appreciation lately for one of the elders or teachers or leaders in the church. Try it, if you have any spikenard in you! It will not likely perfume the whole world—but it won't be forgotten for a long time. "Honor to whom honor is due," says *Romans 13:7*. Sometimes the honor ought to go to those whose work is least prominent. If you have appreciation for someone, break the box today where you are and watch that face light up.

It will spread to *the community*. That is our mission.

"Religion that is pure and undefiled before God is this: to visit orphans and widows in their affliction, and to keep oneself unstained from the world."[4]

"So then, as we have opportunity, let us do good to all men, and especially to those who are of the household of faith."[5]

We are only *talking* about Christ-following much of the time, not doing it. Think. Why can't the *church* be the haven where the transient, or alcoholic, or unwed mother, or bored youth, or frightened businessman, etc. finds love *and* help *and* hope! This is not optional. We *must* break the alabaster box in the community.

WHEN SHALL I BREAK THE BOX

When do we break the box? Mary did not make great plans for the future. She broke the box. She did not wait till time was right to do something earthshaking. She did what she could, right then, with her whole heart, ignoring the cost. Jesus said

> "But if any one has the world's goods and sees his brother in need, yet closes his heart against him, how does God's love abide in him?[18] Little children, let us not love in word or speech but in deed and in truth."[6]

The time is not later, but *now!*

In John Powell's book, *The Secret of Staying in Love,* I found this touching account.

> "It was the day my father died. In the small hospital room, I was supporting him in my arms, when his eyes suddenly widened with a look of awe I had never seen before. Then my father slumped back, and I lowered his head gently onto the pillow. I closed his eyes, and told my mother who was seated by the bedside praying. She startled me. I will never know why these were her first words to me after his death.

> 'Oh, he was so proud of you. He loved you so much.'

> Somehow I knew from my own reaction that these words were saying something very important to me. They were like a sudden shaft of light, like a startling thought I had never before absorbed. Yet there was a definite edge of pain, as though I were going to know my father better in death than I had ever known him in life.

> Later, I was leaning against the wall in the far corner of the

room, crying softly. I couldn't talk through my tears. I wanted to say.

'I'm not crying because my father is dead. I'm crying because my father never told me that he was proud of me. He never told me that he loved me. Of course, I was expected to know these things. I was expected to know the great part I played in his life and the great part I occupied of his heart, but he never told me.'"[7]

Oh, the worth of a token of love. The broken alabaster box.

Now is the time to break that box and give the loveliest of what is in you to Jesus and to all of His sons and daughters.

---

[1] *Matthew 16:24-26.*
[2] Living New Testament, *I John 2:15-17.*
[3] *John 11:35.*
[3] Living New Testament, *Romans 12:1-2.*
[4] *James 1:27.*
[5] *Galatians 6:10.*
[6] *I John 3:17-18.*
[7] See Powell, John. *The Secrets of Staying in Love,* (Niles, Illinois: Argus Communications, 1974), p. 68.

NO LAW FOR CHRISTIANS?
(A Glimpse at Galatians)

You will have discovered that in the Bible truth sometimes is suspended between two poles. At first glance, these poles may appear to be contradictory statements.

In the book of Galatians we have some statements that appear contradictory on the surface. Paul leaves the casual reader wondering "How can we be at once 'under the law of Christ,' yet 'not under law.' He said, "The law was our custodian until Christ came, that we might be justified by faith."[1] He further explains, "We are no longer under a custodian."[2] Therefore, if "the law is the custodian," and we are "no longer under a custodian," we are no longer under the law.

This is further confirmed later in the epistle. "If you are led by the Spirit you are not under the law."[3] The assertion had been made early in the letter as well. "By works of the law shall no one be justified."[4]

The point is clear: we are not "justified by law" nor are we "under law." (See also *Romans 6:14.)*

The apparent contradiction comes in the sixth chapter: "Bear one another's burdens, and *so fulfill the law of Christ.*"[5] This seeming conflict is further complicated by this statement in Paul's Corinthian correspondence. "To those outside the law, I become as one outside the law—not being without law toward God but *under the law of Christ—* that I might win those outside the law."[6] How can it be both ways; "not under law" yet "under the law of Christ"?

I once assumed the word "law" in the book of Galatians referred specifically to the law of Moses or to the Decalogue.

Thus, we would obviously not be under *that* law, but instead under a *new law,* the "New Testament code" called the "law of Christ." Problem resolved! However, as closer examination will show, that explanation proved to be both superficial and inadequate.

In Galatians the word "law" is used thirty times in the English, if I have counted correctly. On twenty of those occasions the definite article does not appear before the Greek word "law." So the original is "law" not *"the* law." In only ten of those cases is the-definite article included to literally say "the law." So Paul is not likely referring exclusively to the old Mosaic law. It would appear the *whole principle* of being "justified by law," *any law,* is to be rejected by the Galatian Christians. This would agree with His message to the Romans. "You are not under law but under grace."[7]

In Colossians we are told that Jesus "canceled the bond which stood against us with its legal demands; this he set aside, nailing it to the cross."[8] This was not referring exclusively to the old Mosaic law, because he says later on: "Let no one disqualify you, insisting on self-abasement and worship of angels, taking his stand on visions, puffed up without reason by his sensuous mind, and not holding fast to the Head."[9] The "law-keeping" he refers to in verse 8 is not the law of Moses, but the keeping of rites and rituals associated with Hellenism and other Gentile cults. No part of the law of Moses could refer to "angel worship," "visions," and the subjective experiences of "the sensuous mind."

So in Colossians and Romans, as well as Galatians, Paul is saying, "Law does not justify," and "we are not under law" (in the sense of being bound and motivated by a mere code of regulations).

What then does "law" mean in *I Corinthians 9:21* and *Galatians 6:2* when we are said to be under the law of Christ?

When we speak of being "not under law", yet "under the law of Christ," we are talking about two different *kinds* of law.

In the term, the "law of Christ, " Paul has reference to a "principle of action." This is a different use of the word "law" from the "code" of specific regulations like the "Gentile rituals" or the Mosaic Decalogue.

We sometimes refer to the "law" of gravity. The law of gravity is not a code rule that you can break. Have you ever tried to violate the law of gravity? You cannot break the law of gravity, it will break you!

We talk about the "law" of diminishing returns. That is not a written injunction—it is simply a principle of the universe. The "law of Christ" to which Paul refers in *Galatians 6:1* is "a principle of life—a principle of action." What is this "principle of action"? It is the nature of the Lord Jesus Christ. It is not a code, but the nature of a person who loves us.

When the apostle Paul uses the word "law" and says you are not under "law," he is talking about a system of Gentile rituals or Jewish traditions, (or any other merely legal system), kept in an· attempt to be justified thereby. "The rules," he is saying, "Can never make people better." It is impossible for the normal human will, left to its own devices, to perfectly comply with divine rules. "For the mind that is set on the flesh is hostile to God; it does not submit to God's law, indeed it cannot; and those who are in the flesh cannot please God."[10] Why? Because cold rules do not change *man's nature*. Man's nature is such that by his own power he will not keep a code of law.

As new creatures, Christians respond to the Lord from a new impulse called "the law of the spirit of life in Christ Jesus."[11]

Jesus changes our natures "in order that the just requirement of the law might be fulfilled in us, who walk not according to the flesh but according to the Spirit."[12]

The primary function of "the law of Moses was twofold. First, it was to point out to us that we were sinners. Second, it was *preparatory,* to get us ready to comprehend the Lord Jesus in our lives. Paul called in "a custodian to bring us to Christ." It was "added because of transgression" until Christ came. *(Galatians 3:19, 24)* But "law" could never save!

THE LAW OF CHRIST

We are saved by grace through faith. We do not *get* saved by law, and we do not *stay* saved by keeping laws. But notice carefully, that when we are justified by grace, it is because we have come to know the Lord Jesus. He captures our hearts. So we place ourselves at his disposal. We will say, "Speak, Lord, your servant hears; command and I will obey." Christians then follow the will of Jesus, not to "get saved" nor for "fear of losing our salvation." We obey him daily *because we are saved.* The Lord Jesus has laid claim on our lives and we have fallen in love with his *nature.* We do what his *nature* would expect. True! Some of the will of Jesus in the New Testament is revealed in His specific commands. But most of it is revealed in His nature. Both His "commands" and his "nature" are embodied in one commandment:

> "A new commandment I give to you, that you love one another; even as I have loved you, that you also love one another. By this all men will know that you are my disciples, if you have love for one another."[13]

He describes what His law is like. It is not a code by which we are justified. It is a principle of life that we follow because we love the Lord Jesus.

Jesus gave a commandment. What was the commandment? "To love—as He loved!" He called it "new." But it was not new in the sense that it had never been heard before. It was heard so long ago, but forgotten for so long that it *seemed* new to them. So he says, "I am writing you a new commandment."

Jesus did not introduce love to the world. That principle has always been in the Father's nature. The Old Testament did not say, "You will be saved if you keep the letter of the law, but it really does not matter what is in your heart." The old law never was meant as a means of justification. Also, God has *always* been concerned, primarily, about the heart. Love has always been central.

The old law served a temporary purpose to show us what sin is and to get us back on the track toward God. But, even in Abraham's day, and until now, men were justified by *faith.* From the beginning God wanted people to trust him and to love their fellow man. It was not a new idea which began with Jesus. So Jesus said, "My 'new commandment' is not really a 'new commandment'

"My 'new commandment' is not really a 'new command-ment' but an old commandment which you had from the beginning." [14]

What then is new about the "new commandment?" What is its difference from the old?

It is *new* because Jesus embodied it. Jesus makes love more clearly understandable because he speaks it as a person. His "law" is not just recorded on some tables of stone, "Love me, and love your neighbor." Jesus has now come and demonstrated how to love by dying. In fact, he says, "Greater love has no man than this: to lay down his life for a friend." That is the "new law."

Now back to Galatians:

"For you were called to freedom, brethren; only do not use your freedom as an opportunity for the flesh, but through love be, servants of one another." [15]

Be servants! Not because of a rule that says you have to, but because of love. "Be servants of one another. For the whole law is fulfilled in one word, 'You shall love your neighbor as yourself.' But if you bite and devour one another take heed that you are not consumed by one another." [16]

Here Paul is saying there is a "new" commandment that

Jesus "brought." There is a "law of Christ." It is not a code kept in an attempt to be justified. It is a principle of action for those who are already justified, so that they can glorify God and be sanctified in their life-style and grow up into Him. It indeed is not a list of rules—do's and don't's. That is not how Jesus changes our natures. But he changes our natures because he has shown us how to love. He called us into *relationship* with Him.

Even if we saw the New Testament as a code of law, a book of rules for the church, it really would not do much to change our hearts. Why should it be easier to keep a set of rules for the church than it was for the Old Testament people to keep a set of rules for Israel? It wouldn't! It was impossible then and it is now. But when the "law" is written in the nature of the Lord Jesus, and the Lord Jesus is in our hearts, that is something else again.

Another problem should be surfaced. Paul said, "If, in our endeavor to be justified in Christ, we ourselves were found to be sinners, is Christ then an agent of sin? Certainly not!"[17] In other words, if people abuse grace, use it as a cop-out from service or as license for the flesh, does that mean grace causes people to sin? Or does it mean that Paul causes people to sin by the kind of gospel he brought? Paul says, "No, no."

But on the other hand, "If I build up again those things which I tore down, then I prove myself a transgressor."[18] That is to say, "If I reinstate 'salvation by the works of law,' I would be transgressing what God wants."

Either way, Paul says, "I'd better not be a transgressor." I had better not reinstate a legalistic system of salvation by keeping rules because that would be transgressing Jesus. And I had better not go right on sinning because "I am saved by grace." That would be transgressing Jesus.

TWO TRANSGRESSIONS

Two distortions of the gospel plagued the early church.

They still dog our heels today. They are legalism and antinomianism.

What is "legalism"? It is what Paul is opposing in the first four chapters of the Galatian letter. Legalism is the notion people are saved by the keeping of a code of law.

Make a clear distinction here: Legalism is *not* the idea that there is a law before which we are responsible. But it is the idea that we are *justified, made right in God's sight by keeping law.*

What is antinomianism? This is what Paul is opposing in the latter part of Galatians, (specifically 5:13 to the end of the letter.) Paul and John both respond to this heresy. Antinomianism is "anti'law'ism." It is the notion that "Since we are justified by grace through faith, *there is no standard* to which we are responsible as a life style." Thus, it turned grace into "an opportunity for the flesh,"[19] and permission to "bite and devour one another."[20] Antionomianism excuses lust, selfishness and back-stabbing.

How do we avoid these "perversions of the gospel"? The secret is in the second chapter of Galatians.

"For I through law, died to law that I might live to God. *I* (my desires, my aims, my will) *have been crucified with Christ."* While the "I" is still alive, it will try to manipulate for its own ends. I did. People who think they are saved by being good are always attempting to put God in their debt. Then they can boast saying, "Ain't I good? I ought to be saved. God, you owe me salvation."

But the word says, "I have been crucified with Christ. It is no longer 'I' who lives, but Christ who lives in me." See! It's Christ living in me. When the "I" dies, Christ takes control. We are now trying to yield ourselves to serve *His* ends. We are no longer trying to use God or to manipulate him. Rather, I am hungry to do what He wants done. When I see how deeply he loves me, His nature becomes appealing.

possible to confuse Caesar and Christ. Discussion of this is easily misunderstood. So there are lilies to pluck in the mine fields. If I should blunder onto a mine, please bury the fragments gently.

This nation began as the beautiful dream of people who wanted to be free. They wanted freedom to do the work they chose to do. Freedom to live where they chose to live. Freedom of private property, of self-expression, and most significantly they wanted freedom for each man to worship God according to his conscience. What beautiful ideals.

As the country grew, it needed further organization and structure. It needed a definitive and well articulated philosophy to shape its direction. The philosophy emerged from leading thinkers of the day, many of whom were heavily influenced by Jesus Christ, others by Greek thought.

From this was formulated the Constitution of the United States, which of course, is the basis upon which the nation is built. It is a uniquely beautiful and valuable document. Few more significant documents have ever been written by human beings.

With time this instrument has gradually gathered around itself a special aura. A spiritual dimension crept into its stature.

History added legend. We know about the Boston Tea party, the American Revolutionary War, and the bitter winter at Valley Forge. We know about the Alamo, Shiloh, Midway and the Battle of the Coral Sea. Legends have produced shrines: Mt. Vernon, Arlington National Cemetery, Washington Memorial, Lincoln Memorial: Places I have gone as an alien to visit with a touch of scorn but came away with tears of emotion in my eyes. These legends and shrines carry powerfully meaningful and moving experiences.

Along with these "legends" and "shrines", we have developed a "national liturgy". The Fourth of July would be the heart of this. At the Kiwanis Club, the Boy Scouts and the Rotary, we recite the Pledge of Allegiance and sing the National Anthem, liturgically reenforcing the American Ideal. This has value. It helps to popularize and perpetuate the beautiful and precious dream.

But finally, through a gradual, strange process of evolution, this complex configuration began to mysteriously, gently evolve upward. It has taken on a "super-human status" until in 1970 a man by the name of Robert Bellah in his book entitled *Beyond Belief* coined a phrase for our feelings. He called this "American Civil Religion". In Bellah's mind a beautiful dream had evolved into a secular religion. Possibly Bellah was unfair. Maybe it is an overstatement to call Americanism "a religion". However there are some aspects of misguided and overzealous patriotism that appear to me to be at deep tension with the religion of the Lord Jesus Christ.

It is explicit in scripture that Christians ought to love their country. I want you to know that while I am an outsider looking in, there's an American flag waving in my yard today. I'm glad to live here. And I'm glad to celebrate this special historic day.

But I am also deeply concerned by some blurring of the lines between Christianity and popular American Ideals. The two are so easily confused and the consequences so easily overlooked.

It is necessary for a country to have some basic beliefs and values shared by everyone. These give stability and direction and cohesiveness. Without such, anarchy would result. However, when these become sacred, Christians have problems.

On our money the words are inscribed, "In God We Trust." Every President has used these words often. Few of them have identified that God personally. We now live in a secularized America. Most Americans do not go to church. God does not have that much to do with their daily lives. Many owe no allegiance to a specific God, especially not

Yahweh, as revealed in the face of Jesus Christ. So the terms, "In God We Trust", or "One nation under God", have become vague deifications of the American ideal and of the state. For some there really is an American civil religion.

What are the basic tenets of that religion? The background philosophy came not as much from the Bible as from the Greek idea that *man is basically good.* If given enough time, enough money and enough education, he can solve nearly any problem. "Everyday and every way the world is getting better." This is not the Christian view of man.

The Bible says that the world, indeed the whole universe is so cursed by the presence of evil that, "All have sinned and come short of the glory of God."[2] Scripture does not teach that we are born "hereditarily and totally depraved". But it does say that all, outside of Jesus Christ, are under the dominion of Satan and are indwelt by "the prince of the power of the air."[3] We are not basically and inherently good. Things are not always going "to get better and better."

For our purposes three basic tenets of American Civil Religion are these:

MY COUNTRY, RIGHT OR WRONG

First, "My Country, Right or Wrong" or, phrased differently, "God is on Our Side." This came rather innocently from a good idea. Obviously, people who had religious faith, when they began an enterprise as important as the building of a nation, wanted to invite God into their plans. So the country was built with God in mind, on principles meant to honor Him. Christian principles. Freedom and justice. Free religion. Free speech! Free enterprise?

The next step led easily to our national direction taking on a sense of divine calling. We became the people with the God-given task of propagating and preserving forever "the imperiled liberties of the world". These "liberties" more specifically emerged as the "free" enterprise system and democratic form of government. The evolution was gradual, but an assumption began emerging that our form of government and our economic system are the only ones totally ordained by God.

Some presidents referred to America as the "Israel of God," with special references to "escape from bondage" to arrive in "the land of promise". The captive chains of Europe were left for the milk and honey of free America. We forgot, however, that there were some free people who were *enjoying their life style* before we arrived. Their human rights were violated in the process of carving out our dream.

The assumption evolved further. Our cause was not only *good,* not merely *blessed* by God, but was *ordained* by God. Finally, in some minds, the attitude formed "whatever is in the interest of the state is really in the interest of God and therefore cannot be wrong." That, in essence makes the state God. Since there is no relevant deity anymore, anyway, and we are living in a "post-Christian era," we worship our "national identity."

Christians cannot accept American civil religion. God is the God of all people. He is on everyone's side—not just ours.

The Bible says, "God so loved the world,"[4] not just America—God, the scriptures say, "unites *all* things in him"[5] (that is in Jesus).

"God has highly exalted him and bestowed on him the name which is above every name, that at the name of Jesus every knee should bow, in heaven and on earth and under the earth, and every tongue confess that Jesus Christ is Lord, to the glory of God the Father."[6]

There is no nation, no national identity, no system of government, no system of economics that in any way can be identified as the *one* that is His. All nations are His. God is the "Ruler of the kings of the earth."

The development of this form of nationalism has led to

some dread distortions. If our aims and objectives were the aims and objectives of God then any means used to perpetuate those aims and objectives are in themselves right. "The ends justify the means." So the CIA could get involved in Chile and do things that, seen through the chronological rear view mirror were atrocious. At the time they appeared to be good and righteous, because they were in the best interest of the country. But what of the interests of the Chileans?

The Vietnamese War, which to many patriots, looked like an unpleasant, but necessary conflict, in retrospect has tarnished considerably.

It shouldn't seem surprising that the principal figures in the Watergate debacle - could say, *and really mean it,* "I did nothing wrong."

"Why?"

"I simply acted in the best interest of the state."

If in the best interest of the state, it is moral to bug the Russian embassy, then if I regard the opposing political party to be subversive to the best interest of America, it is moral for me to bug their national campaign headquarters. I've done nothing wrong!

A person can rationalize any kind of action, if it perpetuates what he believes to be God's will.

Most of us see what is wrong with that. But things can get fuzzy, having been reared in this kind of culture, and when we get emotionally involved with some of our "Christian enterprises."

We need to remember that America is not a theocracy. Jesus is the King of kings and the Lord of lords. He does not just belong to one people.

THE VOICE OF THE PEOPLE IS THE VOICE OF GOD

The second tenet was phrased by the ancient Latins this way, *"Vox populi vox dei."* Translated: "The voice of the people is the voice of God." Where did it come from? The country is built on the concept of democratic government. Beautiful idea! It is fair, it is right that everyone should have a say in government. We all believe in that. So what the majority wants is what we will do.

Next step: Since God is on our side, our objectives are God's objectives, therefore, what most of us decide, is divinely right. Why? Because God's divinely appointed system has so decreed!

The popular American way to decide what is moral is to find out what the majority of the people are doing.

Listen to me, brothers and sisters, students, all of us who need to have this said, if Jesus is Lord, I don't care how many steady but unmarried couples in this town are sleeping together, it is still wrong. We have to remember there are ultimate, transcendent, unchangeable truths. We don't decide what is moral and ethical by asking George Gallup. If the Gallup poll says it is O. K. to go to Southeast Asia and slaughter children, that doesn't make it right. If he says, many Americans commit adultery, it is still sin to commit adultery.

There is a further demonic thing about this method of determining values. First, we take a Gallup poll to find out what everyone believes. Then, not only do we know what most people believe, we get talked into doing these things. After all, if most people in the country think that marriage is temporary, but I think it is permanent, then I'm an outsider and it is un-American of me to be at cross-purposes with the majority. Whatever the majority says is right!

There are absolutes! There are some things that will always be true.

Another strange spin-off is "tentativeness." Since freedom to choose is a sacred right, therefore I *must* exercise my freedom to choose. We have an infinite variety of choices around us. Ladies, if you don't like the color of your hair, Tuesday morning it can be a different color. If any of you guys don't have any hair, Wednesday morning you can have some. Clothing: Any color, size, shape, texture—anything you want. Merchants are selling an infinite variety of everything. The American dream is to make choices, so we exercise this right, changing so repeatedly that we have rendered ourselves incapable of sticking with a decision. Again it's almost un-American to do that. Some even suggest it is emotionally unhealthy to make lasting commitments, irrevocable decisions that don't get changed.

For example, the marriage agreement has become tentative. Shall we commit ourselves to one person, to stay with them no matter how we feel, or whether they are fulfilling our sexual needs or are smoothly compatible? Are we going to work things out under God because we have made a decision? It is easier to say, "I think I will keep the options open."

What about a useful vocation? We live in the age of future shock. Alvin Toffler said most of us will have four or five careers during our lifetimes. So we tend not to get serious about any one career. We are afraid to invest too much of our lives in education for a specific task. As a result, some very valuable ministries are passed by because people are afraid to make the irrevocable commitment necessary to these ministries. We have to keep our options open, exercise our freedom—it's un-American not to be free!

We could multiply examples of this difficulty. But we must confront the biggest decision of all. "Jesus is Lord" has to be remembered as an irrevocable commitment. When we invite people to come down the aisle and say, "Jesus is Lord," if you are a wayward Christian wanting forgiveness, you don't just come to the front to find a temporary guilt release. Come and say, "From this day forward I will be different! I will live for the Lord." Don't play games by using superficial confessions. Come, totally, irrevocably committing yourself to the Lordship of Jesus, un-American or not.

If you have never accepted Jesus, don't be afraid to make that long term commitment.

Let me share something. I have trouble believing! Sometimes I can think of more reasons not to believe than to believe. Sometimes I don't feel like I believe. Sometimes it seems like God doesn't even live in my universe. But, I am believing. I have no plans to quit believing. It doesn't matter how popular it is to keep the options open, I will keep on believing. And I want to call every Christian to do that. Will you do that?

The Christian knows that though everything else changes, there is a changeless God. There is a changeless Christ. He is "The same, yesterday, today and forever."[7] There is "an unshakeable kingdom."[8] There is "the word of God which lives and abides forever."[9] There is rock, brothers.

THE WORK ETHIC/SUCCESS SYNDROME

The third tenet is again the distortion of a good idea. It is the "work ethic" or "success syndrome".

The Bible says, "If a man won't work, he shouldn't eat."[10] The Proverbs are sprinkled with stories about sluggards who go hungry in the winter because they sleep in the summer. The Bible dignifies work. It says, "Whatever your task, work heartily, as serving the Lord and not men, knowing that from the Lord you will receive the inheritance as your reward; you are serving the Lord Christ."[11] "Let the thief no longer steal, but rather let him labor, doing honest work with his hands, so that he may be able to give to those in need."[12] Our fore-fathers valued work and the freedom to work as we wish. They also valued the right to private property. These valuable ideals have been twisted into a two-pronged spiritual hazard.

We easily assume: God blesses a good man. I'll serve God, so that when *I work hard I will get blessed.* People say, "God really blessed my business this year."

"He did? How do you know that He did?"

"Well, I made a lot of money."

Do you think that if He had wiped out your business it could have been a blessing also? You may be in the wrong business? He may have something else in mind for you? He may have had something deeper to teach you about gratitude.

When your business was blessed, how blessed did your employees get? When your income increased five times, did theirs? What are blessings for? If God blesses the hard worker, we work harder in order to make money for us, and *we become the objects of it.*

We Americans tend to evaluate character in the light of ownership. You want to know where the good man is? Look at the man who has a lot of property. But, his "shiftless" neighbor has worked for thirty years and he "hasn't a thing to show for it."

The Mafia owns a lot of property, too, incidentally.

Let me tell you about some good men who have worked for years who don't own very much. You students know a guy by the name of Wendell Broom, don't you? He has blessed thousands of lives. I lean on him. He fills my heart with joy and hope everytime I meet him. He has served and served for more than thirty years, but has he anything to show for it? I'm not even sure his old shoes are paid for. He wears old suits and coats that don't match his britches. Some people laugh at him. They say, "He sure must not have any interest in making something of himself."

Where do we live? What are our values? The Lord said,

"There is great gain in godliness with contentment; for we brought nothing into the world and we cannot take anything out of the world; but if we have food and clothing, with these we shall be content. But those who desire to be rich fall into temptation, into a snare, into many senseless and hurtful desires that plunge men into ruin and destruction. For the love of money is the root of all evils; it is through this craving that some have wandered away from the faith and pierced their hearts with many pangs."[13]

Dr. Wayne Oates, a well-known American counselor, says there are four American addictions. One of them is addiction to alcohol. That's immoral. There is addiction to drugs. That is both immoral and illegal. There is addiction to food. That is neither immoral or illegal, but is very embarrassing. There is addiction to work. That is neither immoral, illegal or embarrassing, rather it has about it an aura of holiness. Thus, some Christians are "workaholics." Their very addiction sanctifies them in our minds. We laud as men of virtue those who have worked themselves to death. Even great spiritual leaders and preachers of the gospel in our minds are often those who worked themselves to death. Where do you see it in the book? Besides being worked to death, a family is robbed of a father, a wife of a husband, neighbors of fellowship, and himself of relaxation and joy. And that is a virtue?

These are by products of the work ethic: To be good, you must be productive of material things. You measure the stature of a man by what he has. Can you not see how terribly distorted that is? How far it is from the religion of the Lord Jesus Christ, even though it is one of the tenets of the American way of life.

Randy Becton summed it up in a little paper that he did on American civil religion. "This tenet of American civil religion says, 'Work hard, go to church, be good to your family, be honest in business.' These are all noble sounding ideas, but they are idolatrous, if they depend on self and on the American ideal or the American presence to accomplish them. They are self-centered and they don't deal with the big issues. They do not deal with guilt, so they never bring peace.

They don't answer the big questions, 'Where did I come from?' 'What is the meaning of my life?' 'What is the meaning of suffering?' 'What is my destiny?' 'How do I cope with death?' 'What is the purpose of my working after all?'"[14]

When Paul wrote these things about "work heartily as to the Lord," "don't worry about what the boss thinks, just work hard," do you know who he was writing to? Slaves! They had absolutely no hope of monetary gain from their work. That could not be their motive. The motive for work is "glory for the Lord." The purpose of having is to give to those who were in need."[15]

THE CHRISTIAN'S RESPONSE

What is the Christian response to all of this? That is important! First, we can't withdraw from it. Christians cannot afford to have no part in civil government because some people have a distorted patriotism into an American civil religion. The Bible says governments should be honored because they are of God.[16]

We should *pay our taxes* gladly because we are paying taxes to support that which is of God, not merely the American government. God lifts one nation up, puts another one down; is sovereign over the nations—all of them. We can't withdraw. We can't stand by wringing our hands and fretting "the condition the country is coming to."

Michelangelo said, "Io critico costruendo, quel cosa de bello." "I criticize by creating something more beautiful." If you don't like what you see, why kick it? Make something so nice that no one will remember the shoddy.

Some positive suggestions for the Christian are clear in the Bible. We can *pray for our rulers.*[17] Prayers are answered. We can *be obedient to law:* all the way from resisting the robbing of banks to honoring the speed limits.[18] We can pay our taxes, "Render to Caesar what belongs to him."[19] We can *honor our rulers.*[20] We can be *salt* and *light* and *leaven* in the world.[21]

But because these things are specifically mentioned in the scriptures doesn't mean that there are no other functions that the Christian has in government.

There are further ways to be "salt and light and leaven." One is simply to *exercise a vote.* An election is taking place. Our society is secular. If there was ever a time when Christians ought to go vote, it is now, this year!

Be involved. Serve. *Don't be afraid to open your mouth on a political or moral issue.* Some may even choose to actually *be a candidate.* Be involved in government.

Yes, it's difficult. And yes, yes, yes, we *Christians are aware no government will ultimately solve problems.* We know that. We know that governments are simply a super-ficial aid to keep society from disintergrating, "keep things between the fences." We know that every time we patch one place, something breaks down in another. We know that government is no ultimate solution because it is human. But we cannot afford to quit.

I sometimes joke with doctors. "Man, why don't you quit. You are losing the battle. Everyone will die sooner or later, in spite of all you do. Why fight it." We wouldn't want them to take that seriously, would we. Sure everyone is going to die, but when I'm sick, I still want someone to help me get well. Now! It is the nature of a Christian to serve and to bless even though he may not see any permanency to the comfort he gives. Jesus went around doing good. So must we.

Jacques Ellul in his book *The Presence of the Kingdom* and again in his book *The New Demons,* says that Christians may feel that being involved in government is futile. It may be like putting a finger into the ocean and removing it again, only to leave no hole. But he opined that God may want a hole in the ocean the size of your finger as long as you have your finger there. Sure when we remove it, the ocean will be unmarked. But right now God may have a place for you to serve and to bless somebody even through a system that we know isn't going to permanently solve any problems.

There is no utopian governmental system. But the Christian can serve.

We must be careful that our children know where the real future is, however.

The other night Carolyn and I took the boys to see "Midway," a nostalgic trip to the World War II Pacific. It was planes and boats smashing and burning each other. At the end there was a scene where the sole surviving American carrier was limping into Pearl Harbor. Everyone was at the docks in victory celebration, waving flags and cheering. Henry Fonda was the U. S. Admiral. The ship was covered with sailors and airmen. Over the bulkhead emerged an admirals cap and there stood Henry Fonda.

John, our son, was sitting beside me. Almost like worship he breathed, "What a great hero!" I thought, "Oh my goodness. What are we teaching kids?" How do I get them to have that kind of feeling about the Lord Jesus? When is he going to sit in church and say, "Wow, wasn't Abraham great?" "Jesus is wonderful." I thought, "How am I ever going to offset the powerful forces of the media that are building the wrong heroes, when I want Jesus to be the hero."

A friend helped me immensely with this problem. He said, "I think your son is smart enough that he will figure out, one of these days, that the Battle of Midway wasn't the world's most important event. He'll see that Henry Fonda is not a U. S. Admiral. He's an old actor. And when the crunch comes, I think your sons will be able to tell whether you are leaning on Fonda or on Abraham's God."

Get that? I want in my life a quality, a center and certitude so my children will know my security is not dependent on the national destiny of the United States or Canada or any country on earth, but in Jesus Christ as Lord. I want them to know that.

SUMMARY

Patriotism doesn't have to be civil religion. It can be a dream of brotherhood from sea to shining sea. How do you get brotherhood to come to be? By waiting on Washington to come out with a better law? By crying when someone runs the flag up? Could we not accomplish more brotherhood by "brothering" someone?

What would you do if tomorrow morning some alien government had taken over the United States. The capital moved from Washington to Denver. The Constitution was scrapped. A new political philosophy is now in its place. You have the same job and the same neighbor. The mountains are the same color and the "golden waves of grain." Could you give your allegiance to that country? Is your gut reaction "Why No! It wouldn't be America."

It wouldn't? It wouldn't be that sacred political entity that is central to American Civil religion, but it would be the same people. It would be the same land. The mountains would be just as beautiful. The same plains as fertile. The land that I love and the people that I serve would still be there. I could give my allegiance to that. It wouldn't matter what you call it. With that as our dream, we can be proud. Proud!

This morning the stars and stripes mean something to us. I'm not ashamed of them. But we can be proud, not that we are part of "God's chosen nation" or that we have "a system designed by God," or that "God is on our side" or that Uncle Sam, the invincible one, will always provide." Rather, we can be proud of the fertile fields, and the beautiful mountains and the good jobs and the peace. Thankful for the free speech and free travel and freedom to worship and the freedom to serve people. The freedom to be what God designed us to be. And we can serve.

I like this country. I don't mind telling you that. It is not my country by birth, but right now it is my country by choice. I am grateful for its ideals and I enjoy its prosperity and freedom. There is a little card in my wallet that says I am a Canadian citizen. But there is a little flag in my front yard that says I'm glad that I live right now in the United States.

I hope that no Christian will re-enforce the shift toward national civil religion today, or any other day. Our real citizenship is in heaven. Our real brothers are all of God's children everywhere in the world. Our real Lord and Chief of State is Jesus Christ. Our real land is "across Jordan." (This one is just a place we're passing through on a pilgrimage.) The Lord is already constructing a place for us in our permanent land. Our real flag is the blood-stained banner of the Prince of Peace. We can praise Him for that.

We render to Caesar the things that are Caesars and to God the things that are God's. But as for me and my house, not very much belongs to Caesar, and even Caesar is under the sovereignty of God.

---

[1] *Matthew 22:15.*
[2] *Romans 3:23.*
[3] *Ephesians 2:1-4.*
[4] *John 3:16.*
[5] *Ephesians 1:10.*
[6] *Philippians 2:9-11.*
[7] *Hebrews 13:8.*
[8] *Hebrews 12:28.*
[9] *I Peter 1:25.*
[10] *II Thessalonians 3:10.*
[11] *Colossians 3:23-24—Ephesians 6:6-7.*
[12] *Ephesians 4:28.*
[13] *I Timothy 6:6-10.*
[14] Randy Becton-"A Work Ethic"-October, 1975.
[15] *Ephesians 4:28.*
[16] *Romans 13:1-7.*
[17] *I Timothy 2:2.*
[18] *Romans 13:1.*
[19] *Matthew 22:21.*
[20] *I Peter 2:17.* '
[21] *Matthew 5:13-16.*

20th CENTURY SERMONS

PURCHASE PLAN

To those who purchase the first eleven volumes of 20th CENTURY SERMONS, volume XII will be given free of charge when the original purchaser completes and mails in the eleven different certificates bound in the back of each volume, according to the instructions given below.

This plan will afford a substantial saving and will also be a convenience for those who wish to receive each volume as it comes from the press without placing a new order each time. By filling in the order blank at the bottom of the opposite page and returning it to your bookseller, each new volume of the remainder of the first eleven books will be delivered to you upon its publication.

Since publication will be at four month intervals, the cost will be distributed over a long period, so that in effect it will be like buying on the installment plan and will not require a strain upon one's budget at any one time.

Not only will this plan be a convenience and a saving but it will assure your obtaining the complete set of the very best sermons of twelve great gospel preachers of our day.

Follow these instructions to claim your free copy of Volume 12

INSTRUCTIONS

1. After you have purchased all of the first eleven volumes, remove the certificate from each book. One is bound in the back of every volume sold.
2. Sign each certificate on the line provided for your name. Be sure to sign all eleven. Do not include certificates signed by another person. They are non-transferable.
3. Enter your mail address on the certificate for Volume 1.
4. Arrange the certificates in numerical sequence from Volume 1 to Volume 11 with the certificate for Volume 1 (bearing your present address) on top.
5. Clip or pin the certificates together.
6. Mail them to the publishers, Biblical Research Press, Abilene, Texas, to arrive not later than November 30, 1978. It is not necessary to write a letter.
7. After you mail your certificates to the publishers your free copy of Volume 12 will be mailed to the address you provide on the certificate for Volume 1.

PLEASE DO NOT REQUEST REDEMPTION

1. If you have not purchased each of the eleven volumes, or if they have not been purchased for you.
2. If you do not have a valid certificate from each of the eleven volumes so purchased. Lost certificates will not be honored—no exceptions.
3. After November 30, 1978.

Volume 12 is scheduled to be available in the Summer of 1978.

DO NOT REMOVE THIS CERTIFICATE
UNTIL YOU HAVE PURCHASED THE TEN OTHER VOLUMES

THIS certifies that the undersigned is the original purchaser of this Volume X (ten) of 20th Century Sermons and is entitled to receive with the compliments of his bookseller a copy of Volume XII provided he shall have purchased, not later than four months following publication of Volume XII, one copy each of Volumes I to XI inclusive and shall have sent to his bookseller at one time signed certificates for each volume so purchased.

VOL. X

1. This certificate is of value only to the original purchaser of Volume X; it is non-transferable.
2. The schedule of publication provides for publication of three volumes each year beginning October 1968 and continuing until Volume XII is published in the summer of 1978. This certificate will be invalid after November 1978, unless extended by reason of delayed publication of Volume XII.
3. In event this publication schedule is extended, the right to do so being reserved by the publishers, the expiration date of this certificate will be extended likewise.
4. This certificate is of no value unless signed by the original purchaser and accompanied by the appropriate certificates from each of the ten other volumes specified above, each also signed by the same original purchaser.
5. This certificate is the only evidence of purchase acceptable for redemption under this offer.

I certify that I am the original purchaser of this Volume X of 20th Century Sermons and submit herewith the appropriate signed certificates from each of the other ten volumes as required above. Please send me without charge my complimentary copy of Volume XII.

NAME ....
Address ....
City .... State .... Zip ....

ORDER BLANK

FOR THE 20th CENTURY SERMONS SERIES

To: (Bookseller) ....
. . . .
. . . .
Please send immediately the following volumes of 20th Century Sermons, and each succeeding volume as published, at $5.95 per volume:

...... Vol. I ...... Vol. VII Signed ....
...... Vol. II ...... Vol. VIII Mail Address..................
...... Vol. III ......Vol. IX City.........................
...... Vol. IV ...... Vol. X State .... Zip ....
...... Vol. V !..... Vol. XI
...... Vol. VI ...... Vol. XII ( ) Cash Enclosed ( ) Bill Me
( ) I expect to use the 20th CENTURY SERMONS Purchase Plan Certificates to receive Volume XII free.

Published by
BIBLICAL RESEARCH PRESS, 774 E. N. 15th, Abilene, Texas 79601